Why Read This Book?

The last major bipartisan tax reform was enacted in 1986, more than 30 years ago. Since then, many politicians, policymakers, and think tanks have developed bipartisan tax reform proposals. None have been enacted. So what makes the ideas in this book any different?

Rational Tax Reform proposes a totally new approach (systems engineering) to achieve nonpartisan tax reform. Systems engineering (SE) is a proven process that engineers use to develop complex products such as aircraft and spacecraft. It uses facts and data to optimize a product or system. This book is based on a revolutionary idea—that SE can be used to optimize social, economic, and political systems as well as physical products and systems.

You should read this book if you are interested in (1) how SE can fix America's broken tax system, or (2) how SE can address other urgent social, economic, and political problems beyond tax reform. The following comments from reviewers are offered to help you decide if this book is for you.

Reviewer Comments

"This book is clear and lucid. It succeeds beautifully in demonstrating how rationalizing one part of the system (the tax system) can be the key to addressing many other vexing problems such as health care, social inequality, and climate change. I see lots of opportunities to deploy the same SE approach to other social systems." — Dr. Saif Benjaafar, Distinguished McKnight Professor and Head, Department of Industrial and Systems Engineering at the University of Minnesota College of Engineering and Science

"I am seriously impressed with this book and the proposed tax reform. I like the practical, nonpartisan SE approach to tax writing. I strongly agree with the tax reform proposal except for a few small differences. Now let's get these ideas to tax writers, federal and state." — T. R. Reid, *New York Times* bestselling author of *A Fine Mess: A Global Quest for a Simpler, Fairer, and More Efficient Tax System* and *The Healing of America: A Global Quest for Better, Cheaper, and Fairer Health Care*

"The SE process is so powerful and logical, I wonder why politicians are not already using it to develop government policy." — Stephanie Hoogstad

"The proposed tax reform is ingenious. Send a copy to the president and every member of Congress." — Suzie Housley

"This book infuses practicality, logic, and dynamism into the normally dry subject of tax reform. It makes tax reform interesting." — Kit Duncan

More Reviewer Comments

Organization and Content

This book is organized as follows:

Chapter 1 describes the systems engineering (SE) process and discusses how it is used to develop spacecraft and aircraft.

Chapters 2 through 6 use SE to develop a comprehensive tax reform proposal that simplifies the tax code, balances the federal budget, encourages economic growth, and addresses urgent social, economic, and political issues.

Chapter 7 provides a detailed plan that lawmakers can use to refine this tax reform proposal, implement nonpartisan tax reform, and continuously improve the tax code.

Chapter 8 provides a summary and discusses the path forward. Specifically, it identifies actions that I am taking and that you and others can take to jump-start tax reform and fix America's broken tax system.

Chapter 9 describes how lawmakers and policymakers can use SE to address other social, economic, and political problems beyond tax reform.

> This book contains about 30 figures and tables that are not easy to read on a smartphone or small tablet. For best results, the ebook should be read on a tablet or computer whose screen size is at least six inches by eight inches. If you do not have access to a tablet or computer with this screen size, I recommend you purchase the paperback rather than an ebook.

Rational Tax Reform

Using the
Systems Engineering Process
to Fix America's Broken Tax System

Jim Hartung

Rational Tax Reform:
Using the Systems Engineering Process to Fix America's Broken Tax System
By Jim Hartung

1. BUS064000 2. POL024000 3. LAW086000
Paperback ISBN: 978-1-949642-31-5
Ebook ISBN: 978-1-949642-32-2

Cover design by Lewis Agrell

Printed in the United States of America

Authority Publishing
11230 Gold Express Dr. #310-413
Gold River, CA 95670
800-877-1097
www.AuthorityPublishing.com

Table of Contents

The tax code is a statement of a country's values, so it is also a statement of your values and the legacy you want to leave for future generations. As you read this book, think about how tax reform will affect your children, grandchildren, America, and the world.

This book is dedicated to my wife Carol, our children Stacie and Justin, their spouses Lucas and Emily, and our grandchildren Olivia and Austin.

PREFACE

America's tax system is a mess. It is complex, inefficient, and riddled with loopholes. It does not address urgent problems such as the increasing national debt, inefficient and inadequate health care, unsustainable Social Security, deteriorating infrastructure and education, and inequality of income and wealth. For decades, lawmakers have been unable to fix the tax code because of ideological differences. They need a better process to achieve bipartisan tax reform.

Systems engineering (SE) can help lawmakers develop innovative nonpartisan solutions that bridge the partisan divide. Engineers use SE to develop complex products such as aircraft and spacecraft. SE is a systematic process that seeks to balance opposing interests, conflicting objectives, and many constraints. It considers the needs of all stakeholders and finds optimum solutions.

I selected the title *Rational Tax Reform* since my goal is to develop a "rational" approach to taxation and tax reform. Rational means logical, reasoned, sensible, prudent, cogent, practical, pragmatic, sound, judicious, and intelligent. Those words are seldom used to describe the tax code. Rational tax reform is definitely a "stretch" goal. Nevertheless, often the best way to make progress is by setting an audacious goal that requires "thinking outside the box."

I chose engineering for my profession since I like the precision of mathematics, the exploration of science, and the practicality of building things. I have nearly 40 years' experience as a systems engineer, manager, and executive in the aerospace and energy industries. For most of my career, I worked for Boeing, United Technologies, and Rockwell International. As a result, when I began writing this book, I had detailed expertise in SE and general knowledge of economics, government policy, taxes, health care, and politics. Writing this book has expanded my understanding of these subjects, especially in the areas of tax policy and health care.

You may wonder why I am interested in tax reform. It's because I believe our (broken) tax system is a root cause of many of America's most serious economic, social, and political problems. To address these problems, we must eliminate the root cause. This requires fundamental and comprehensive tax reform.

As I wrote this book, I realized that SE can be used to address many other societal problems in addition to tax reform. I included one chapter (Chapter 9) to briefly discuss the process. I have also developed a website (jimhartung.com) with more information. If you are interested in using SE to address societal problems beyond tax reform, I suggest you read this book first, because it provides an easy-to-follow example that illustrates the process. Then, visit my website for additional information.

"Briefing Book" Format

This book uses a "briefing book" format. Each page has a title on top with its key message. Each page also includes text, bullets, a table, a figure, or a picture to support or explain the title. Some pages also include a dialogue box with supplementary information. I used this format for three reasons:

- The briefing book format is easy to read since each page is a complete "packet" of information. You can read and assess each page on its own merits rather than wading through many pages looking for supporting information.

- This format facilitates discussion, which is essential to the SE process. You can discuss this book one page at a time while looking at a hard copy, viewing it on a computer, or projecting it onto a large screen.

- The briefing book format allows this book to be briefed to politicians, policymakers, and others who are interested in tax reform.

So, as you read this book, imagine you are the president or a member of Congress receiving this proposal to fix America's broken tax system.

My goal in writing this book is to describe the SE process and how lawmakers can use it to reform and improve the tax system.

To keep this book short and concise, I have included only enough background information so a knowledgeable reader can understand the SE process and the proposed tax reform. The glossary defines key terms and acronyms and provides supplementary information regarding GDP (Gross Domestic Product) and the national debt.

Readers who want more information on the current U.S. tax system, the history of taxation, tax systems used by other countries, and tax reform alternatives should consider reading one or more of the six books on tax reform cited in the bibliography. For a general overview of tax reform, one of the best books is *A Fine Mess: A Global Quest for a Simpler, Fairer, and More Efficient Tax System* by T. R. Reid.

Of course, readers who want the most up-to-date information on taxes and related subjects should search the Internet. For a general overview of taxes and tax reform, two of the best resources are the websites of the Peter G. Peterson Foundation and the Tax Policy Center.

Tax Reform Should Be Bipartisan

Systems engineering (SE) considers the needs of all stakeholders. Therefore, it is inherently bipartisan (and nonpartisan). My goal is to define a tax system and reform process that Republicans, Democrats, Independents, and others can all support.

Most Republicans want to control spending, limit the size of the government, and reduce the national debt. Unfortunately, neither Republicans nor Democrats have done a good job of controlling federal expenditures in the past few years. This has led to large deficits. As a result, the national debt is growing unsustainably. Tax reform must address this problem. The proposed tax reform balances the budget, controls spending, and reduces the national debt.

Most Democrats want more (and better) government services, especially universal health care, improved education, increased infrastructure investment, and sustainable Social Security benefits. Democrats generally want to pay for these services by increasing tax rates for high-income taxpayers. Republicans worry that raising tax rates will stunt economic growth. Tax reform must reconcile these differing opinions. The proposed tax reform funds universal health care, protects Social Security benefits, and increases funding for education and infrastructure without reducing other government services, raising tax rates, or increasing the burden on taxpayers.

Independents agree with Republicans on some issues and Democrats on other issues. Often, they are frustrated with both major political parties. The proposed tax reform is a unique combination of conservative and liberal ideas, as well as several new ideas that I believe will appeal to Independents and others, including Libertarians and Green Party members.

Nearly all taxpayers want a simpler and fairer tax system that encourages growth and creates jobs. Unfortunately, conservatives, liberals, and moderates disagree on how to do this. Tax reform must resolve these differences. I have attempted to do this by offering a bold but rational new approach to taxation and tax reform.

The image on the cover of this book (the Republican elephant and Democratic donkey) illustrates my objective that tax reform should be bipartisan.

The image on the right is used to denote the first page of each chapter. It is a reminder that my objective is fair, balanced, and nonpartisan tax reform.

Tax Reform Should Address America's $100 Trillion Debt Problem and Improve the Health Care System

The Congressional Budget Office (CBO) projects that the national debt owed to the public will grow from about $17 trillion in late 2019 to nearly $30 trillion in 2029 and $100 trillion by 2049—only 30 years from now.

(Note: The total debt, including debt owed to other agencies of the federal government, was $23 trillion in late 2019. The glossary provides more information on the national debt.)

The large and growing national debt will seriously degrade the lives of most Americans. It will crowd out other needed investments, make U.S. businesses less competitive, reduce job opportunities, and decrease America's power and influence in the world. As the debt grows, it will require painful cuts to Social Security, Medicare, defense, and other government services.

My goal is to balance the federal budget without increasing the burden on taxpayers or reducing government services. To do this, waste must be eliminated somewhere in the economy. The easiest target is health care, since the U.S. spends twice as much on health care as other developed countries. By reforming the health care system, we can provide better health care and reduce cost.

In the past 10 years, Congress and the president have enacted two landmark laws to fix the health care and tax systems. Democrats enacted the Affordable Care Act (often called ObamaCare) in 2010 and Republicans enacted the Tax Cuts and Jobs Act (TCJA) in 2017. Both laws fixed a few obvious problems, but neither achieved fundamental reform. My goal is to reform both the health care and tax systems at the same time, using a "systems" approach.

Since tax reform and health care reform are both difficult, wouldn't it be easier to tackle them one at a time? No! They are synergistic, so it is easier to reform them together. Tax reform is needed to fund health care reform. Health care reform is needed to reduce health care costs and balance the federal budget. By implementing both at the same time, we can improve health care, reduce its cost, and balance the federal budget without increasing the burden on taxpayers.

Health care reform should be bipartisan, like tax reform. My plan to reform the health care system is similar to Medicare-for-All popularized by progressive Democrats, but different because it includes two key features that most Republicans and Independents want: (1) strong cost controls, and (2) an opt-out provision. I call my plan "Medicare Choice" because everyone will have a choice. They can choose Medicare—or opt out and receive premium support for any health care insurance they prefer.

Insights from the Reagan Tax Reforms
(Why We Need Tax Reform Now)

President Reagan signed two major tax bills during his administration: the Economic Recovery Tax Act of 1981 and the Tax Reform Act of 1986.

The 1981 legislation was primarily a tax cut, hastily enacted by Republicans without bipartisan support. It stimulated economic growth. Unfortunately, it also increased the federal deficit and the national debt. Shortly after its passage, President Reagan and Congress recognized the need for more tax reform.

After a lengthy bipartisan process, Congress and President Reagan enacted the Tax Reform Act of 1986. It simplified the tax code, reduced deductions, and lowered marginal tax rates. After that reform, the U.S. tax code was considered one of the best in the world. Many countries reformed their tax laws based on its principles.

Since then, other countries have continued to improve their tax systems, while the U.S. tax system has become more complex and inefficient. To address this problem, Republicans enacted the Tax Cuts and Jobs Act (TCJA) in late 2017, without bipartisan support. This act reduced the corporate income tax rate from 35% to 21% and made other changes to encourage companies to invest in the U.S. rather than overseas. It also reduced individual income taxes by lowering tax rates, increasing the standard deduction, and limiting itemized deductions.

Some Republicans believe the TCJA will pay for itself over the long term with increased growth. Most economists and Democrats think it will increase federal deficits and the national debt. Regardless of who is right, fundamental tax reform is still needed as the TCJA was mainly a tax cut rather than tax reform, and it did not address most of the problems with the current tax code.

The TCJA of 2017 is similar to the Economic Recovery Tax Act of 1981, in that both were tax cuts enacted by Republicans to stimulate economic growth. Neither achieved comprehensive tax reform. Just as President Reagan and Congress passed the bipartisan Tax Reform Act of 1986 to fix the problems that were not addressed in the 1981 law, Congress and the president should enact bipartisan tax reform now to fix the problems the TCJA did not address.

1 THE SYSTEMS ENGINEERING (SE) PROCESS

Systems engineering (SE) is a systematic, multi-disciplinary approach for the design, development, implementation, and operation of a system. SE seeks a balanced design in the face of opposing interests and many frequently conflicting objectives and constraints.

SE is often a process of discovery. Systems engineers begin by discovering the key problems that must be resolved and identifying the best ways to solve them.

Engineers have developed many tools to assist with the SE of complex products such as aircraft and spacecraft. However, since the tax system is relatively simple and straightforward (it's not rocket science!), no special expertise is required to "systems engineer" the tax code.

Figure 1-1 shows the SE process, simplified and adapted for tax reform. It includes six blocks, or steps. The organization of this book follows this flow chart, with one chapter for each block.

Key subjects such as the national debt, health care, and Social Security are examined multiple times, once for each block in the flow chart. This allows them to be explored from different perspectives and in increasing detail to find the best solutions. Although this may feel a bit repetitive, that is how the SE process works. It solves a complex problem (like developing an aircraft, spacecraft, or tax system) by breaking it into a series of small repeatable steps.

Figure 1-1. The SE Process for Tax Reform

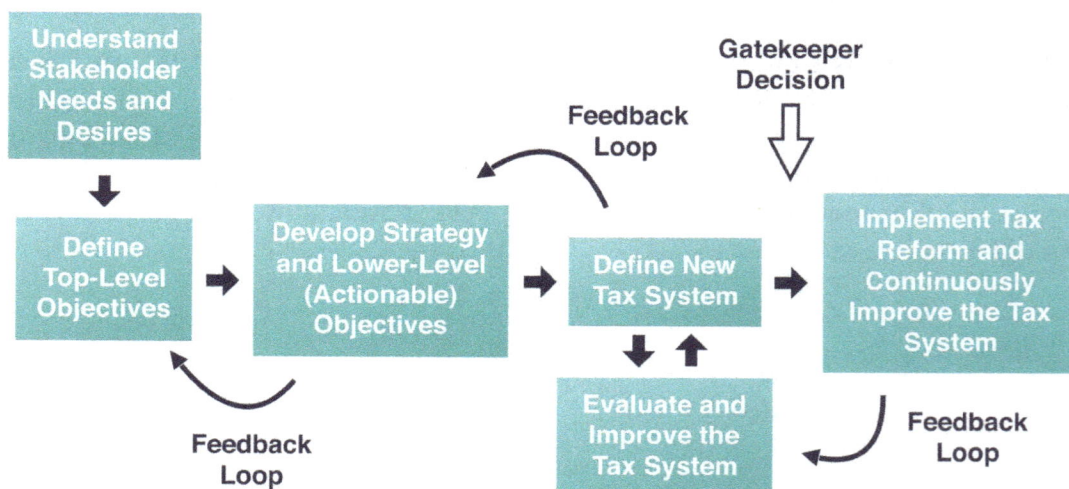

Is Tax Reform Too Complex and Political to Benefit from the SE Process?

No! SE has been used successfully on extremely complex and political programs such as the International Space Station (ISS). SE does not resolve political conflicts, but it does provide a systematic and logical process to discuss and resolve conflicts.

The ISS has operated successfully in orbit for more than 20 years. It is by far the largest spacecraft ever built. It weighs 925,000 pounds and is 360 feet long. Its crew of six live and work in a pressurized volume that is roughly equivalent to a Boeing 747 aircraft. Each day, it completes 16 orbits and travels the equivalent distance of going to the moon and back. The ISS was assembled in orbit from 1998 to 2010, using 36 Space Shuttle flights and five Russian launch vehicle flights.

SE allowed engineers and managers to harmonize and manage the diverse objectives, opinions, and capabilities of 15 countries: the United States, Russia, Canada, Japan, and 11 European nations (Great Britain, Germany, France, Spain, Italy, Belgium, Denmark, Norway, Sweden, Switzerland, and the Netherlands).

Figure 1-2. International Space Station (ISS)

Photo courtesy of NASA.

The SE Process for the International Space Station

Understanding how SE was used to build the ISS will shed light on how SE can be applied to tax reform. Figure 1-3 shows the SE process for the ISS; note the similarities with Figure 1-1.

The ISS had many stakeholders: Congress, the president, the American public, international partners, and various groups within NASA (e.g., astronauts, science researchers, and engineering groups). The stakeholders had many diverse objectives. For example, some groups within NASA wanted a relatively small (low-risk) space station, while other groups wanted a large space station that would significantly advance state-of-the-art developments in science, technology, and space exploration. The Clinton administration wanted to employ as many Russian scientists and engineers as practical in a peaceful, cooperative effort so they would not be employed building and proliferating nuclear weapons. The Russian Space Agency wanted cash directly from NASA since the Russian government at that time was too poor to adequately support their space program.

The SE process had to reconcile these diverse views and define top-level requirements that stakeholders could agree upon. Then these top-level requirements had to be flowed down and allocated to every ISS program element, system, module, assembly, and component. For the entire ISS, this required thousands of requirements documents and specifications. All requirements had to be traceable from the top-level documents to the lowest-level specifications and verified through testing, analysis, or inspection.

Figure 1-3. SE Process for the International Space Station

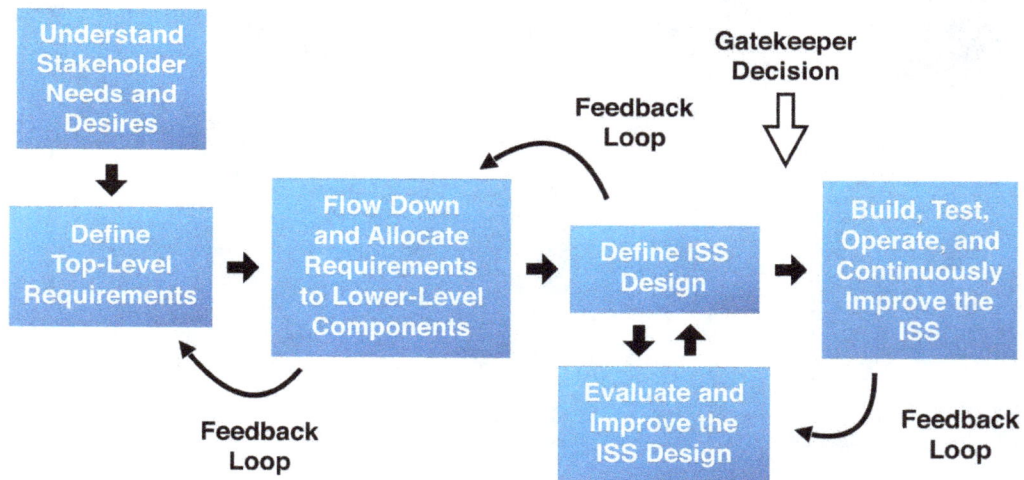

The SE Process for the International Space Station (continued)

After ISS requirements were established, the next step in the SE process was to define the design. For the ISS, the design process was difficult and time-consuming since many new technologies had to be developed or improved upon. This required extensive development and testing since designers need accurate and reliable engineering data to achieve their objectives.

Three major events complicated the ISS design and implementation process. The first was the collapse of the Soviet Union in 1991. Before then, the U.S. was developing a space station (Freedom) with Europe, Japan, and Canada—and Russia was developing its own space station (Mir). After the Soviet Union collapsed, the U.S. and Russia decided to join the two space stations into one (the ISS). This significantly delayed the program but in the long run, provided many advantages.

The other two events were (1) the loss of the Space Shuttle Columbia in 2003, about halfway through ISS assembly, and (2) the termination of the Space Shuttle Program in 2011. After the Columbia accident, the shuttle fleet was grounded for 30 months and ISS assembly was delayed 40 months. While the shuttle fleet was grounded from 2003 through 2006 and after the Space Shuttle Program was terminated in 2011, Russian launch vehicles provided ISS crew launch, return, and logistics support.

The ISS was able to survive these setbacks in large part because of the SE process. When the Soviet Union collapsed, SE provided a disciplined approach to integrate the Russian and U.S. space stations. In general, the best features of the Russian Mir design were combined with the best features of the U.S. Freedom design. Safety was enhanced by retaining both U.S. and Russian flight-critical safety systems and launch vehicles, so each could be a backup for the other.

Lawmakers need a robust process such as SE to help them overcome problems and achieve success. Fortunately, the tax system is far less complicated than the space station, so the SE process for tax reform is much simpler. Nothing new needs to be invented for the tax system. The tax systems in the U.S. and in other countries comprise an excellent laboratory in which to formulate alternative tax systems. We can select the best ideas and improve on them, rather than develop totally new (and unproven) approaches to taxation.

SE Is an Iterative Process

SE is an iterative process, especially for complex products. Systems engineers cycle through the first five steps of the SE process several times to develop and optimize a design. The reason is simple: it is impossible to fully define requirements without exploring design alternatives. For example, NASA and its international partners used four major iterations to develop the ISS design. The first two iterations were as follows:

- **Pre-conceptual design:** NASA developed the pre-conceptual design themselves. In this effort, they focused on understanding stakeholder needs and desires, defining top-level objectives, and selecting a "reference" design concept.

- **Design concept:** Next, NASA hired eight contractors to further develop the space station design. I was working for Rockwell International at the time, and NASA selected us and another contractor to (independently) develop the electric power system design concept. We performed dozens of studies to develop the design concept, define top-level requirements, identify key problems, and develop strategies to resolve them.

After developing the design concept, NASA selected three contractors to develop and build the ISS. Rockwell International was chosen to develop the electric power system. We developed the design in two major steps:

- **Preliminary design:** In this phase, we defined the design in enough detail to identify specific requirements and interfaces for all components. We also developed and tested engineering models and software to support the design effort. This phase culminated with a major "Preliminary Design Review."

- **Detailed design:** Once the preliminary design was complete, we defined the detailed design and prepared manufacturing drawings. To support this effort, we developed and tested additional engineering models and software. This phase culminated with a "Critical Design Review."

After completing the design, we manufactured "qualification" and "flight" hardware and tested it to ensure that it met requirements. Once the hardware and software were proven at the component level, they were integrated into larger assemblies and tested again. This process continued until the ISS was integrated in orbit.

The foregoing is a simplified explanation of the iterative SE process. One reason tax reform has failed in the past is that Congress and the president have not used an iterative process. Typically, they designate a group to develop a tax reform proposal, which is usually dead on arrival, for a variety of reasons. They do not use an ongoing, iterative process to develop and refine tax reform proposals. Chapter 7 provides a roadmap for how they could do this.

SE Requires Both Facts and Judgment

Engineers know how to work with facts. Just as a spacecraft or aircraft designed with incorrect facts will not fly, a tax system based on faulty information will not achieve its intended objectives. The tax system should be based on solid, provable facts, not ideology. This is the approach taken here.

SE also requires good judgment. Here are two examples:

- Boeing developed the 777 aircraft with two engines rather than four to reduce manufacturing and operating costs. This was a risk since the FAA had not yet approved two-engine aircraft for long flights over water. Boeing's judgment proved correct. The 777 demonstrated its reliability during early flights and the FAA approved extended operation over water (far away from the nearest airport).

- Boeing developed the 787 aircraft with carbon fiber composites to reduce weight and fuel consumption. This allows the 787 to serve very long-distance, point-to-point markets. This was a risk as many people thought hub-and-spoke flights would dominate future commercial air traffic. Boeing's judgment again proved correct. The 787 reduced fuel costs and its long non-stop flights are more popular and profitable than hub-and-spoke flights.

These two decisions were controversial when Boeing made them. Nevertheless, it is not surprising that these judgments proved correct as they were based on facts and data rather than ideology or other subjective criteria. These decisions allowed Boeing and its airline customers to grow and prosper. They have also made air travel better and cheaper.

To compete globally, the U.S. should learn from Boeing's decisions on the 777 and 787 aircraft. Their bold and well-informed decisions transformed the airline industry. Now, comprehensive tax reform based on solid facts and informed judgment could energize and revitalize America.

Lessons Learned from the Boeing 737 Max Crashes

The Boeing 737 MAX was grounded in March 2019 after two fatal crashes. Since Boeing uses SE to develop its aircraft, it is vital to investigate whether these accidents indicate a flaw in the SE process.

The 737 MAX is the fourth generation of the 737 aircraft. The first three generations entered service in 1966, 1984, and 1996, and the MAX was introduced in 2017.

Boeing originally planned to replace the third-generation 737 with a "clean-sheet" design. However, in 2011, Airbus launched the A320neo (new engine option). Within six months, Airbus had sold more than 1,000 aircraft, setting a record and taking sales away from the 737. To meet Airbus' challenge, Boeing abandoned its plan to develop a clean-sheet aircraft and instead created the MAX by upgrading the third-generation 737 and installing new, larger, more efficient engines.

Boeing decided to mount the new (larger) engines forward and upward from the wings rather than increase the aircraft height enough to accommodate the engines under the wings. As a result, the 737 MAX's nose pitches upward when engine thrust is increased.

To prevent a stall, Boeing added a maneuvering characteristics augmentation system (MCAS). The design of the MCAS relied on a single angle-of-attack instrument. When that instrument failed (as it did in both accidents) and erroneously indicated that the aircraft was about to stall, the MCAS repeatedly commanded the nose down.

Boeing did not include a description of the MCAS in the flight crew operations manual, which is the basis for airlines' documentation and training. As a result, flight crews did not train for MCAS failure, did not realize that MCAS failure could cause a crash, and did not know how to recognize and recover from MCAS failure.

These problems suggest serious flaws in Boeing's management and SE processes during the 737 MAX's development. As expected, Boeing is taking action to improve its management and SE processes. The 737 MAX crashes did not raise questions about the value of the SE process itself; rather, they showed how failure to rigorously apply the SE process can lead to extremely negative consequences.

Lawmakers and the public are (justifiably) critical of Boeing for these crashes and the process failures that led to them. However, in their zeal to criticize Boeing, lawmakers should realize that the lessons learned apply to them as well. Congress and the president need to develop robust bipartisan processes (such as SE) to effectively govern the country. The broken tax, health care, immigration, justice, and education systems should spur them to action and cause them to improve their processes, just as Boeing is taking action to improve its processes.

2 STAKEHOLDER NEEDS AND DESIRES

All taxpayers are stakeholders. Defining stakeholder needs and desires requires a systems engineer to be inquisitive, open to new ideas, and non-ideological. Often, stakeholders don't know what they want. In this case, systems engineers must ask probing questions to help stakeholders understand their needs and desires.

Stakeholder needs and desires should be defined broadly enough to include the diverse views of most taxpayers, yet specific enough to guide the SE process. Here are a few of the most important stakeholder needs and desires, which we will explore in greater detail in the following pages:

- Make government more efficient, control spending, and balance the federal budget. Reduce tax rates and the burden on taxpayers without cutting essential services.

- Encourage economic growth. Create more good jobs, especially for low-income and middle-income taxpayers, and reduce inequality of income and wealth.

- Simplify the tax system and make it fairer. Reduce opportunities and incentives for tax avoidance, tax evasion, influence peddling, and corruption.

- Improve the health care system. Reduce the cost of health care and expand coverage. Protect Medicare benefits and reform Medicaid.

- Restore Social Security to financial health without cutting benefits.

SE Process for Tax Reform

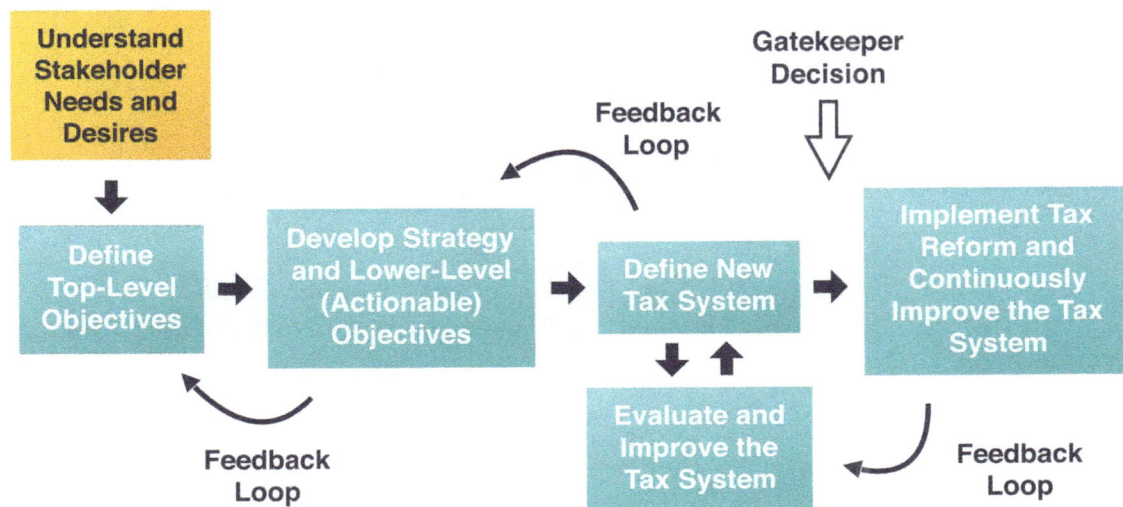

Stakeholders Want to Reduce the Federal Deficit

Figure 2-1 shows the federal budget deficit. It increased from $400 billion in 2015 to nearly $800 billion in 2018. The CBO (Congressional Budget Office) estimates it will grow to $1 trillion in 2021 and $1.4 trillion by 2028. These deficits will add $12 trillion to the national debt over the next 10 years. The debt will grow even faster if the U.S. enters a recession.

Although not shown here, the CBO projects that the federal deficit will grow to $3 trillion annually in 20 years and $6 trillion annually in 30 years. This will add $35 trillion to the national debt in 20 years and $80 trillion to the national debt in 30 years.

Stakeholders want to control spending and balance the federal budget without cutting essential government services or increasing tax rates.

Figure 2-1. Federal Budget Deficit Is Large and Increasing

Annual Deficit (Billions of Dollars)

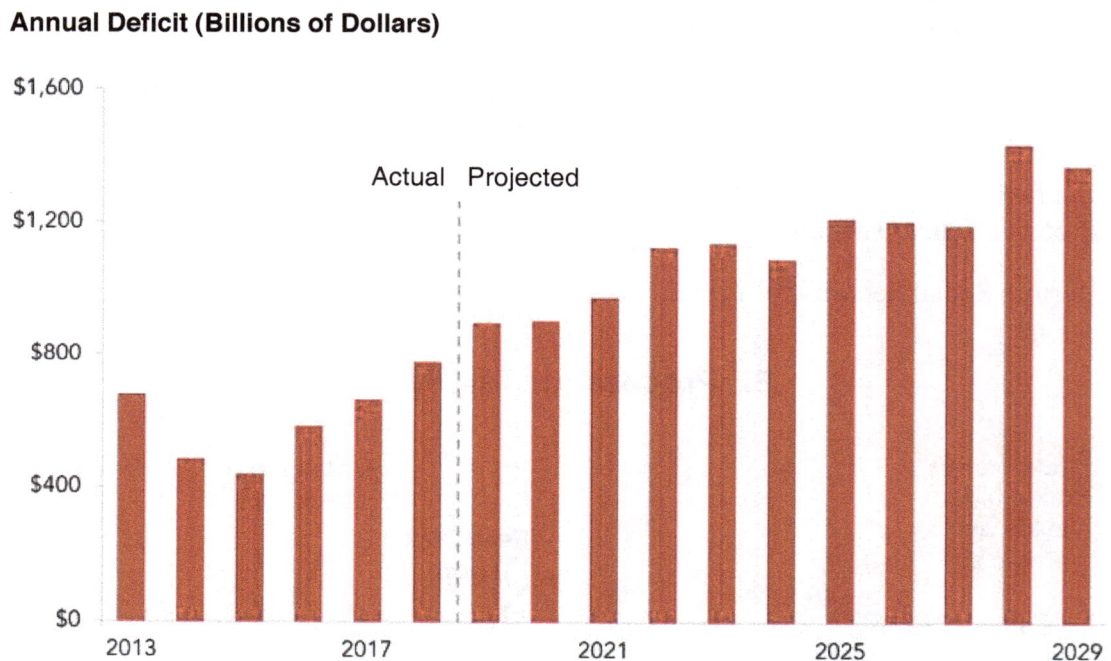

Source: Congressional Budget Office, *The Budget and Economic Outlook: 2019 to 2029,* January 2019. Compiled by the Peter G. Peterson Foundation and used with their permission.

Stakeholders Want to Reduce the National Debt

Both the Congressional Budget Office (CBO) and the Department of the Treasury believe the federal debt is on an unsustainable path. Figure 2-2 shows why. Historically, the U.S. has carried fairly low debt, except in times of crisis. Now, the debt is growing rapidly, even with a good economy. This is unprecedented.

For most of the past 50 years, the national debt owed to the public was less than 40% of GDP (Gross Domestic Product). It is now 78% of GDP. The CBO projects that the debt will grow to 144% of GDP over the next 30 years.

Spending is growing much faster than revenue for three reasons: (1) the aging population, (2) increased health care spending, and (3) rising interest on the debt. The CBO projects that the federal deficit will grow to nearly 9% of GDP in the next 30 years. The deficit will then be one-half of tax revenue. In other words, the federal government will be like a family who spends 50% more than their income.

Although not shown here, the CBO projects that the debt could grow faster—to more than 200% of GDP in 30 years—and the Department of the Treasury projects that it will grow to 350% of GDP in 50 years. When interest on the debt consumes most tax revenue, the U.S. will be essentially bankrupt.

Stakeholders want to reverse this trend and reduce the national debt.

Figure 2-2. National Debt Is Growing Unsustainably

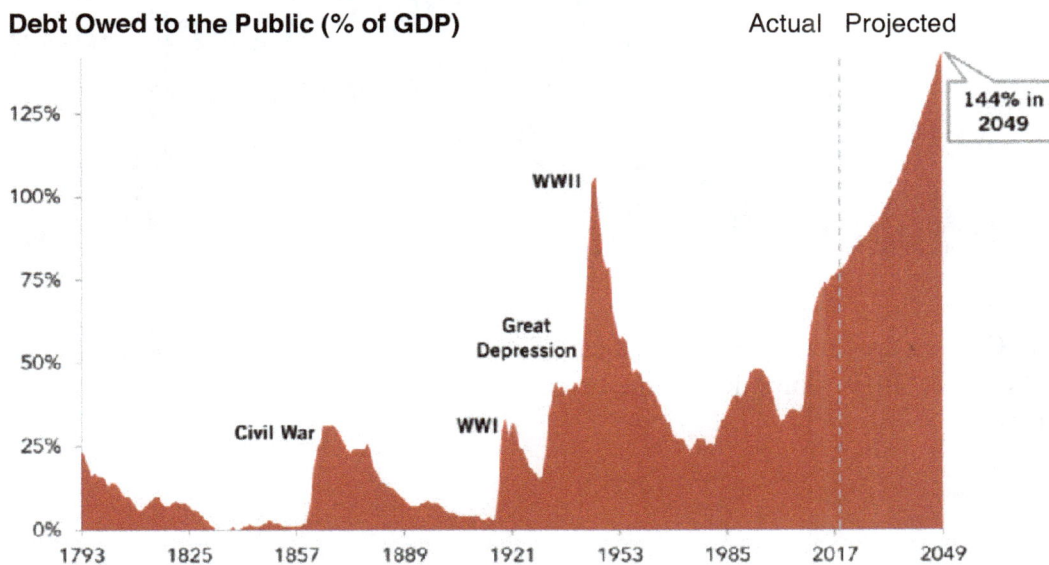

Source: Congressional Budget Office, *The 2019 Long-Term Budget Outlook,* June 2019. Compiled by the Peter G. Peterson Foundation and used with their permission.

Stakeholders Want to Improve the Health Care System

Figure 2-3 shows U.S. health care expenditures since 1960 and projected growth in health care costs.

Health care expenditures increased from 5% of GDP in 1960 to almost 18% of GDP in 2017. Some of this increase is due to our aging population, but most is due to problems with our health care system. The Centers for Medicare and Medicaid Services projects that health care expenditures will grow to nearly 20% of GDP in 10 years.

Other developed countries spend an average of 9% of their GDP on health care. Even with their lower expenditures, they provide universal health care and achieve longer average life expectancies.

Stakeholders want a better and lower-cost health care system.

Figure 2-3. Health Care Expenditures Are Increasing Rapidly

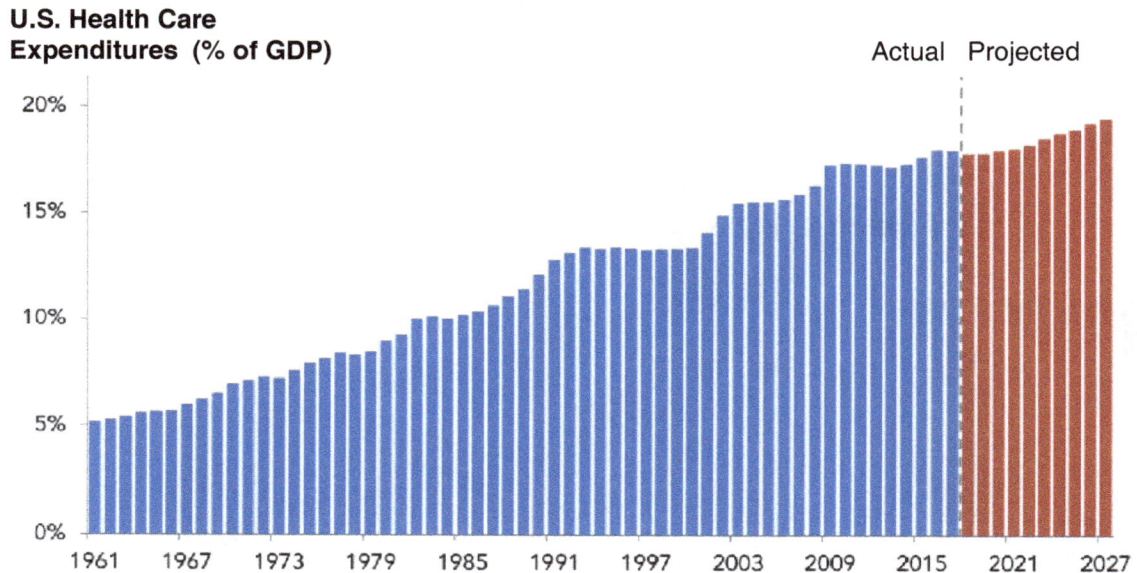

Source: Centers for Medicare and Medicaid Services, *National Health Expenditure Data,* February 2019. Compiled by the Peter G. Peterson Foundation and used with their permission.

Examples of Waste and Inefficiency
in America's Health Care System

The U.S. health care system encourages some people to have costly medical treatments of questionable value while others have no health care. Here are two examples of wastefulness in the health care system:

- **Example #1:** When my father-in-law was 95 years old, he was diagnosed with leukemia. His oncologist recommended chemotherapy. A second doctor recommended hospice instead, as he thought my father-in-law had less than one month to live, and chemotherapy would make him miserable without any significant benefit. My father-in-law agreed with the second doctor and two weeks later he passed away. My wife and I are sure hospice was more appropriate for her father than chemotherapy. Unfortunately, many people might have taken the first doctor's recommendation because our society conditions us to preserve life, regardless of cost or pain and suffering. When doctors recommend measures to prolong life, it is difficult for loved ones to reject that advice. And too often, families encourage doctors to prolong life at all cost, even when the treatment is inappropriate.

- **Example #2:** My mother-in-law was diagnosed with dementia when she was 90 years old. Two years later, after her dementia had advanced considerably, a heart specialist recommended a major operation to fix a partly clogged valve in her heart and install a pacemaker. She told her doctor she did not want to undergo a major operation. He persisted, telling her she could die suddenly if she did not have the operation. She told him, "That doesn't sound so bad." When I asked the doctor if he knew that my mother-in-law had dementia, he said, "Yes, but don't you want the best possible quality of life for your mother-in-law?" I told him that the operation might actually degrade the quality of her life, especially in the short term. My mother-in-law chose not to have the operation, and lived two years longer. The best medical help she (and we) received was not from high-cost specialists, but from a nurse practitioner who provided practical advice on how to deal with dementia.

These examples are cited not to denigrate U.S. medical professionals, who as a group are among the best in the world. They nevertheless illustrate the absurdity and wastefulness of our current health care system.

These are not isolated instances. Most people I know can cite examples of waste, inefficiency, unfairness, inconsistency, and other problems in our health care system.

Stakeholders want to reduce waste and inefficiency in the health care system.

Stakeholders Want to Restore Social Security to Financial Health

Social Security benefits are a major source of retirement income. They are especially important for low-income and middle-income taxpayers.

Unfortunately, Social Security is not sustainable as currently defined. Figure 2-4 shows how Social Security will deplete its $2.9 trillion trust fund in 15 years. If no action is taken before then, Social Security benefits will have to be reduced by more than 20%.

Stakeholders want to restore Social Security to financial health without cutting benefits.

Figure 2-4. Social Security Trust Fund Will Be Depleted in 15 Years

Social Security Surpluses and Deficits (% of GDP)

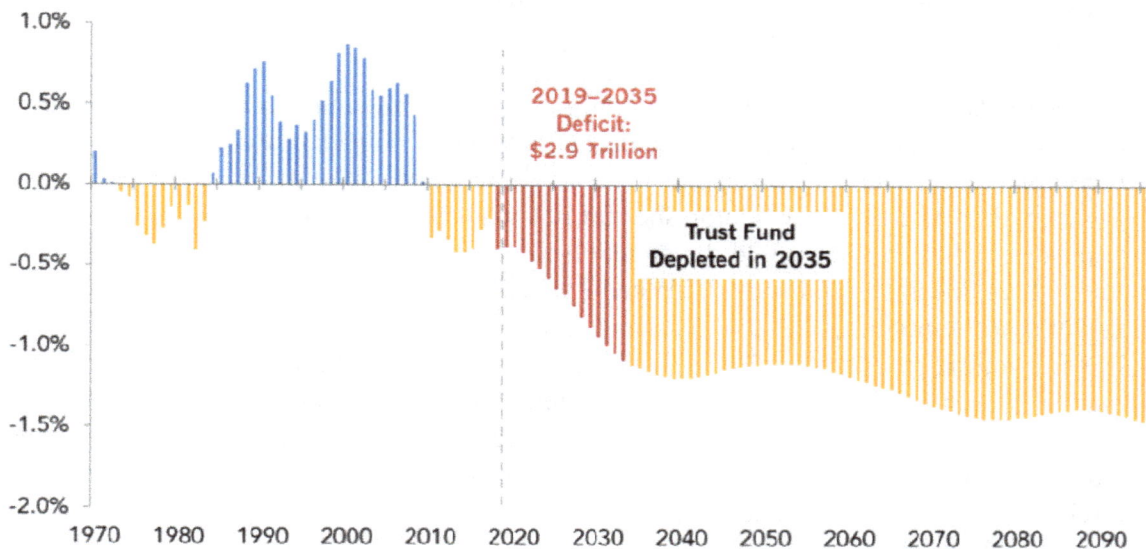

Source: Social Security Administration, *The 2019 Annual Report of the Board of Trustees of the Federal Old-Age and Survivors Insurance and Federal Disability Insurance Trust Fund,* April 2019. The surpluses and deficits exclude interest income. The $2.9 trillion deficit is the present value of the cash deficits between 2018 and 2034. Compiled by the Peter G. Peterson Foundation and used with their permission.

Stakeholders Want Better Opportunities
for Low-Income and Middle-Income Taxpayers

Wealth in the U.S. is distributed unequally, and that inequality is increasing. Table 2-1 shows how wealth inequality grew from 1980 to 2018. As a result, the top 1% of households owned 37% of all wealth in 2018 and the bottom 90% owned only 27% of all wealth. Wealth has not been distributed this unevenly since the Great Depression.

The tax code cannot solve the problem of inequality, but it should at least try to level the playing field. This is a challenge. Children born into wealthy families and those with loving and nurturing parents, unique talents, good brains, and healthy bodies start life with better opportunities than those who are not so fortunate.

For most of our history, Americans have believed that anyone, regardless of where they were born or what class they were born into, can attain their own version of success through hard work and perseverance. This "American Dream" is in danger of extinction for too many people. A fair, efficient, fiscally responsible, and growth-oriented tax system can help restore it. The best way to address the problem of inequality is by providing (1) better opportunities and incentives for low-income and middle-income taxpayers to move up the income ladder, and (2) a strong social safety net.

Creating good opportunities for everyone is important, both for humanitarian reasons and because society will benefit from useful, productive, and happy citizens. Good jobs provide good incomes. Just as important, they enhance self-esteem and enable upward mobility.

Stakeholders want better opportunities for everyone, but especially for low-income and middle-income taxpayers.

Table 2-1. U.S. Wealth Inequality Is Large and Increasing

Household Wealth	Share of Wealth (%)		Increase (%)
	1980	2018	
Top 0.01%	3%	10%	233%
Top 0.1%	7%	20%	186%
Top 1%	22%	37%	68%
Top 10%	60%	73%	22%
Bottom 90%	40%	27%	-33%

Source: *The Triumph of Injustice* by Emmanuel Saez and Gabriel Zucman, and *Global Wealth Inequality*, Paper 25462, National Bureau of Economic Research, by Gabriel Zucman. Compiled by the author.

Stakeholders Want a Simple, Fair, and Efficient Tax Code

The federal tax code is roughly 3,000 pages long and contains hundreds of tax deductions, credits, preferences, and loopholes. To fully understand the tax code requires mastery of about 70,000 pages of supplementary regulations and case law. The IRS estimates that taxpayers spend more than six billion hours annually preparing tax returns.

Tax deductions, credits, preferences, and loopholes in the current tax code allowed taxpayers to (legally) avoid $1.5 trillion in taxes in 2018. In addition, the IRS estimates that taxpayers (illegally) evade taxes worth more than $400 billion annually. So together, legal tax avoidance and illegal tax evasion totaled $1.9 trillion in 2018. Coincidentally, all individual and corporate income tax revenue in 2018 was also $1.9 trillion. This is a remarkable fact: tax avoidance and evasion in the current tax system is equal to all individual and corporate income tax revenue.

A simple, fair, and efficient tax code would provide the following advantages:

- Reduce the time spent preparing tax returns.

- Decrease opportunities and incentives for tax avoidance, tax evasion, and corruption.

- Allow taxpayers to make decisions based on economic merit rather than to reduce taxes.

Taxpayers want a simpler, fairer, and more efficient tax code.

"The art of taxation consists of plucking the goose to obtain the largest amount of feathers with the least amount of hissing."

— Jean-Baptiste Colbert

Colbert was a French politician who served as the French Minister of Finance from 1661 to 1683 under King Louis XIV. When he made this statement, he was probably thinking that French citizens were the geese from whom he wanted to extract the largest amount of taxes with the least amount of hissing.

However, a better way to read this quote is by considering the economy as a goose that lays golden eggs. We want a simple, fair, and efficient tax system that will not disturb the goose (the economy) so it will continue laying golden eggs and even increase production.

Stakeholders Want Bipartisan Tax Reform

President Reagan's top domestic priority in his second term was tax reform. He achieved this with passage of the Tax Reform Act of 1986. Working with Speaker of the House Tip O'Neill, a Democrat, they developed a tax reform bill that achieved roughly two-to-one bipartisan support. The actual voting went as follows:

- Senate Republicans: 79% favor, 21% oppose

- Senate Democrats: 73% favor, 27% oppose

- House Republicans: 65% favor, 35% oppose

- House Democrats: 70% favor, 30% oppose

This shows that bipartisan tax reform is possible. For important bills like tax reform, the goal should be to achieve at least two-to-one bipartisan support, as this suggests the reform meets the needs and desires of most taxpayers.

Most stakeholders want Congress and the president to enact bipartisan tax reform.

Steve Kelley Editorial Cartoon used with the permission of Steve Kelley and Creators Syndicate. All rights reserved.

3 TAX REFORM OBJECTIVES

The next step in the SE process is to define top-level objectives. The objectives should capture stakeholder needs and desires succinctly and accurately. The Peter G. Peterson Foundation has developed good top-level objectives for tax reform, so they are used here:

- **Fiscally responsible:** Tax reform should balance the federal budget and reduce the national debt.

- **Pro-growth:** Tax reform should support economic growth, productivity, and competitiveness.

- **Realistic:** Tax reform should be evaluated with realistic assumptions.

- **Comprehensive:** Reform should be comprehensive—tax cuts are not tax reform.

- **Fair:** The benefits of tax reform should be widely shared with the most economically vulnerable protected.

- **Simple:** Tax reform should simplify the tax code.

- **Permanent:** Reform should enact permanent changes to the tax code.

- **Bipartisan:** Bipartisan tax reform is more durable and long-lasting.

SE Process for Tax Reform

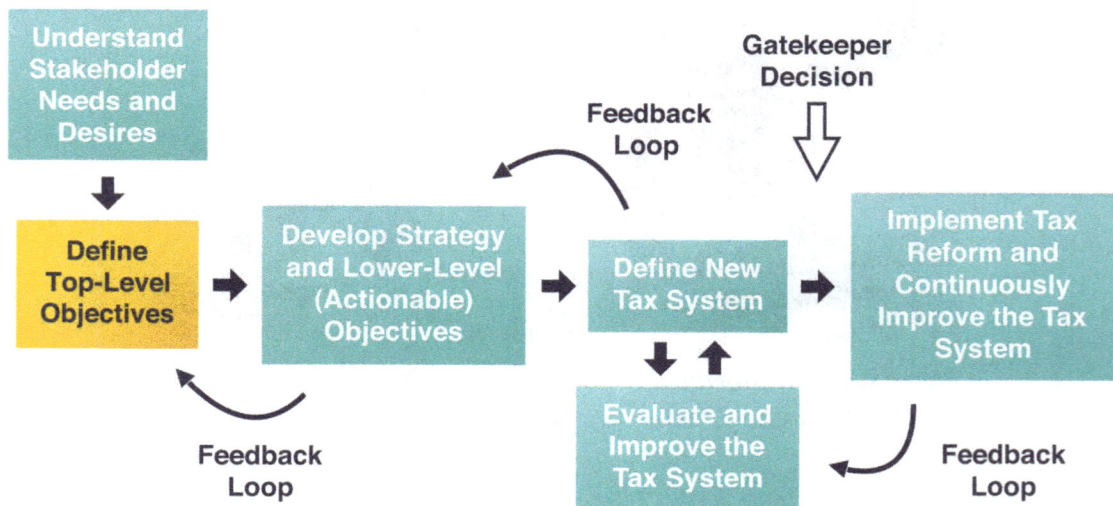

4 STRATEGY TO ACHIEVE OBJECTIVES

The eight objectives on the previous page are too general to define a new tax system. They must be transformed into lower-level (actionable) objectives, which requires a strategy. The following pages present one strategy to achieve the top-level objectives.

Several alternative strategies should be considered before selecting one. Sometimes the best strategy is obvious; sometimes it is not. When the best strategy is not obvious, the first five steps of the SE process must be completed for two or more strategies in order to select the best one for implementation.

To develop a strategy, a systems engineer examines the big picture first and asks fundamental questions such as these:

- How much tax revenue does the federal government need to perform its required functions?

- What is the best way to obtain this revenue and ensure the government does not overspend?

- What strategy can best achieve all eight tax reform objectives?

These questions are subjective, and different people will provide different answers. Nevertheless, quantifying the answers enables an informed discussion of the alternatives.

SE Process for Tax Reform

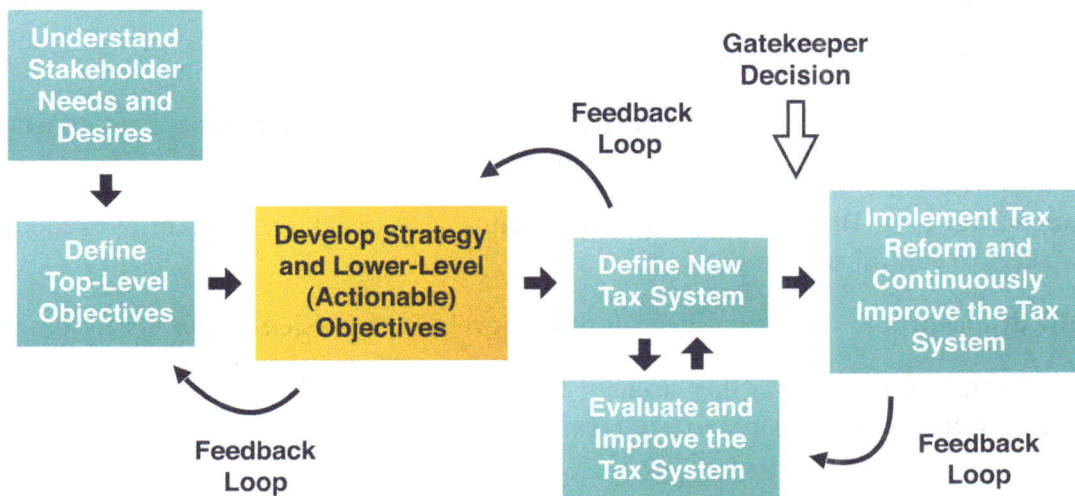

Tax Reform Strategy

The tax reform strategy proposed here is similar to the strategy used to develop the bipartisan Tax Reform Act of 1986. That act broadened the tax base, reduced tax rates, and fixed other problems with the tax code. The tax reform strategy proposed here broadens the tax base for all three major taxes—individual and corporate income taxes and the payroll tax. It also includes health care reform to decrease the cost of health care. This allows tax rates to be reduced and still provide sufficient revenue to fund Medicare Choice, restore Social Security to financial health, increase funding for infrastructure and education, and address other current problems. The key features of the proposed strategy are as follows:

Individual income tax: Broaden the tax base and reduce tax rates.

- Tax all sources of income at the same (progressive) rates with fewer tax brackets and lower tax rates.

- Eliminate itemized deductions and increase the standard deduction.

- Provide a refundable tax credit for every taxpayer and dependent. Eliminate all other tax credits.

Corporate income tax: Replace the corporate income tax with a broader and more efficient value-added tax (VAT) with a lower tax rate.

- Earmark all VAT revenue to fund Medicare Choice. Implement cost controls to keep the VAT tax rate as low as is practical.

Payroll tax: Eliminate the cap on taxable income and reduce the tax rate.

- Earmark all payroll tax revenue for Social Security (no diversion for Medicare).

Estate tax: Use estate tax revenue to improve the education system.

Excise taxes: Index motor vehicle fuel taxes for inflation. Add a new revenue-neutral excise tax (carbon dividends) to address climate change.

Balanced budgets: Balance the budget and include a feedback mechanism to encourage lawmakers to control spending.

Public disclosure: Require candidates for high-level office to release their tax forms.

The following pages discuss this strategy in more detail and describe how it is used to develop lower-level (actionable) objectives.

What Is a Value-Added Tax?

The value-added tax (VAT) is similar to a sales tax, except that it is collected from businesses at each step of the production process rather than at the time of the final sale. Businesses pay the VAT based on their "value added," which is the difference between their sales and the cost of goods purchased.

Businesses calculate their VAT based on total sales, but receive a credit for VAT paid by their suppliers. This credit is given to avoid taxing a product or service more than once. However, as a side benefit, businesses are incentivized to pay the VAT to avoid being "frozen out" of the supply chain.

The VAT is the world's most common consumption tax. Many European countries enacted VATs in the 1960s and 1970s. Other countries followed in the 1980s and thereafter. It is now used by more than 160 countries around the world, including all developed countries except the U.S.

The VAT is a popular form of taxation for several reasons: (1) it is easy to administer, (2) it creates few negative economic distortions, (3) it raises lots of money, (4) it encourages savings and investment by shifting part of the tax burden from income taxes to consumption taxes, and (5) it allows border adjustments for imports and exports.

Several prominent U.S. politicians have proposed a VAT as a replacement for corporate income taxes. For example, former House of Representatives Speaker Paul Ryan's "business consumption tax," Senator Ted Cruz's "business flat tax," and Senator Rand Paul's "fair and flat tax" are all VATs with slightly different names and assumptions.

The tax reform proposed here replaces the corporate income tax with a VAT and earmarks all VAT revenue to fund Medicare Choice. Earmarking VAT revenue to fund Medicare Choice has five major advantages: (1) it provides a reliable funding stream for Medicare Choice, (2) it prevents politicians from diverting funds to other (less important) programs, (3) it allows taxpayers to see clearly how their VAT dollars are being spent, (4) it creates a de facto limit on spending for Medicare Choice, and (5) it enables Medicare Choice to continue, even if Congress and the president cannot agree on an annual budget.

Why Replace the Corporate Income Tax with a Value-Added Tax?

The corporate income tax is complex. It is relatively easy to avoid and often causes companies to make poor business decisions merely to reduce taxes. A value-added tax (VAT) is more difficult to avoid. It is a better way to tax corporate profits as part of a broad-based consumption tax.

Eliminating the corporate income tax avoids the problem of double-taxing corporate profits (once through the corporate income tax and again as capital gains and dividends). This simplifies individual income taxes, as it allows capital gains and dividends to be taxed as ordinary income.

The corporate income tax, for all its problems, is only a small source of government revenue. Corporate income in the U.S. has varied from roughly 5% to 10% of GDP for the past 70 years. Therefore, a corporate income tax rate of 21% (the current rate) generates tax revenue of about 1% to 2% of GDP (0.21 x 5% to 10%).

Eliminating the corporate income tax will stimulate economic growth. Other developed countries are reducing their corporate income tax rates. By eliminating the corporate income tax, the U.S. will lead rather than follow this trend.

The proposed tax reform replaces the current 21% corporate income tax with a broad-based VAT with a 13% tax rate. This tax rate was selected to provide sufficient revenue to fund Medicare Choice.

The VAT envisioned here is similar to New Zealand's "Goods and Services Tax." New Zealand adopted this tax over 30 years ago, and since then, their tax rate has varied between 10% and 15%.

All major developed countries other than the U.S. have both a corporate income tax and a value-added tax. Their average corporate income tax rate is slightly over 20%, and their average VAT tax rate is slightly less than 20%.

With the proposed tax reform, the U.S. will have a lower VAT tax rate than most other developed countries and no corporate income tax.

Why Implement Medicare Choice with Strong Cost Controls?

The current U.S. health care system is an inefficient hodgepodge of disjointed programs: Medicare, Medicaid, and thousands of other health care and insurance programs. As a result, U.S. health care expenditures are twice those of other developed countries.

In spite of our higher health care expenditures, many people in the U.S. are uninsured and cannot afford adequate health care. All other developed countries provide universal health care for their citizens.

High health care expenditures are damaging the competitiveness of U.S. companies and straining the budgets of federal, state, and local governments. They are also a problem for individuals and families; health care cost is a leading cause of personal bankruptcies.

Medicare is popular. It provides health care for U.S. citizens over 65 as well as some younger people. The simplest and most effective way to improve the U.S. health care system and reduce total (public and private) expenditures is to expand Medicare to cover all age groups and implement strong cost controls.

The Medicare Choice proposed here is different from most Medicare-for-All proposals because it includes strong cost controls and an opt-out provision. The cost controls are designed to reduce the total cost of health care. The opt-out provision allows individual taxpayers and groups of taxpayers (for example, employers and unions) to purchase insurance from any health care provider they choose and receive premium support from the government. Both features are discussed in more detail later.

Some people may object to Medicare Choice because they think it is "socialized medicine" where the government provides free health care. The Medicare Choice proposed here is not socialized medicine for two reasons:

- Private industry (not the government) provides all health care. Private health care providers and private insurance companies are not eliminated in the proposed Medicare Choice system.

- Taxpayers pay for Medicare Choice with the VAT, just as they currently pay for Medicare with payroll taxes and general tax revenue.

Under Medicare Choice, the federal government will be involved in health care decisions, as it is now. Americans accept government involvement in other aspects of our lives, such as laws and regulations. That is not socialism.

A Brief History of Medicare

Medicare was first implemented in Saskatchewan, Canada, in 1944. Its key features were (1) universal health care, (2) private health care providers, and (3) a single-payer (the government). Medicare was popular in Saskatchewan, so by the mid-1960s, Canada enacted Medicare nationwide (for everyone) and the U.S. enacted Medicare for seniors aged 65 or over. Medicare has operated in the U.S. for a half-century, during which it has undergone several changes. Three of the most important are:

- Coverage has been expanded to cover people younger than 65 who have qualifying disabilities, end-stage renal disease (requiring dialysis), and amyotrophic lateral sclerosis (ALS).

- Medicare Advantage was added. It allows Medicare to contract with health maintenance organizations (HMOs) and preferred provider organizations (PPOs) to provide comprehensive health care.

- Prescription drug coverage was added to Medicare benefits.

One common misconception is that Medicare limits the choice of health care providers. This is not true. Medicare provides two major options. Those who want to choose their own doctors can sign up for "Original Medicare" and those who prefer a comprehensive health care organization can enroll in "Medicare Advantage." Medicare offers more freedom of choice than most private insurance plans and does not require a change of doctors when one changes employers.

In the 1990s, Taiwan wanted to improve their health care system, so they formed a commission to study the systems in developed countries and identify the best one for Taiwan. The commission rejected the U.S. health care system. Instead, they recommended a Medicare system similar to Canada's, with a centralized database similar to France's and cost control measures similar to Japan's. Their system provides universal health care for less than one-half the cost of U.S. health care.

We can learn much from other countries. Their citizens generally like their health care systems, except for two issues: (1) countries without adequate cost controls end up rationing usage through long wait times, and (2) countries with draconian cost controls threaten the financial viability of their health care providers.

The Medicare Choice envisioned here strikes a balance between those two extremes. It includes strong cost controls to limit expenditures and encourage taxpayers to use the health care system wisely. However, the cost controls are not so strong that they will prevent people from obtaining health care when they need it or drive good health care providers out of business. Of course, inefficient and poor health care providers will be forced to improve if they want to survive.

Medicare Choice Cost Target = 14% of GDP

Figure 4-1 shows health care expenditures in major developed countries and the proposed Medicare Choice cost target. The key items to note in this figure are:

- The U.S. spends far more on health care than other major developed countries. We spent about 17% of GDP and $10,600 per person in 2018. Other major developed countries spent between 8% and 12% of their GDP and between $3,000 and $6,000 per person. (Note: U.S. health care expenditures in Figure 4-1, which is based on OECD data, are slightly lower than those in Figure 2-3, which is based on CMS data.)

- The proposed Medicare Choice cost target (14% of GDP) is roughly halfway between current health care expenditures in the U.S. and other major developed countries. This objective is achievable, given other developed countries spend much less.

Although not shown here, life expectancy in the U.S. is 2.5 to 5.5 years shorter than in other major developed countries (*OECD Health Statistics 2019*). Over the next four pages, we discuss how Medicare Choice can improve health care and reduce cost.

Figure 4-1. Medicare Choice Cost Target

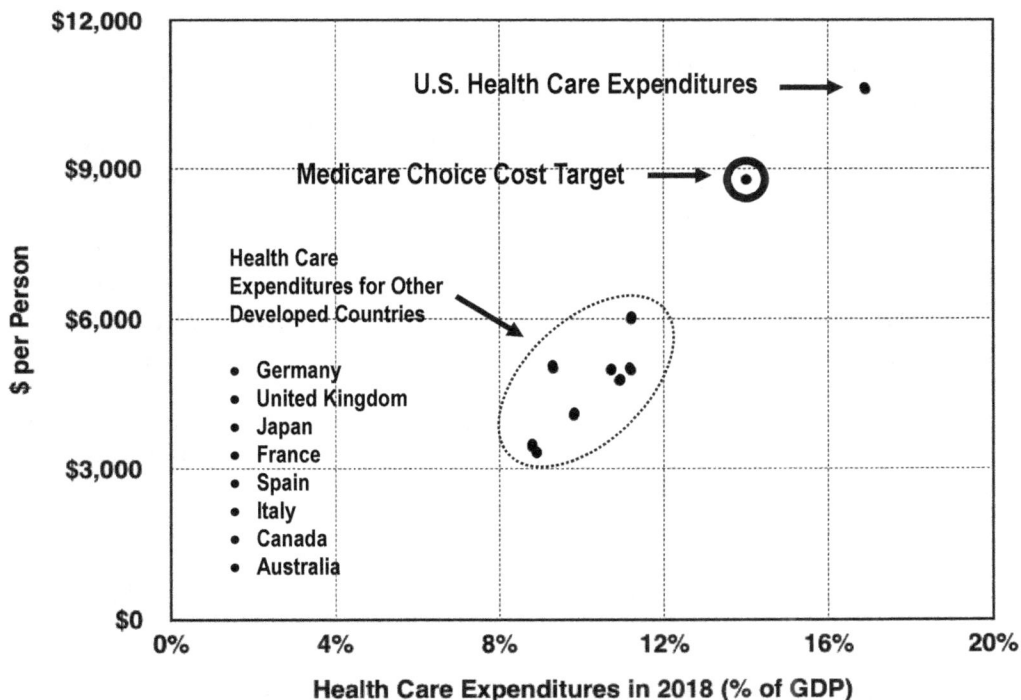

Source: Organization for Economic Cooperation and Development, *OECD Health Statistics 2019,* June 2019. Data are for 2018 or latest available. This figure uses purchasing power parity to convert data into U.S. dollars. Compiled by the author.

Medicare Choice Can Reduce Cost
and Improve Health Care

Medicare Choice should be managed like a company with clear cost and health care improvement targets, a board of directors, and annual reports. Their goal should be to provide the best possible health care within the cost target established by Congress and the president, rather than the best health care at any cost.

It will be much easier to manage a single health care system like Medicare Choice than the current hodgepodge of health care systems, which is practically unmanageable. Among ways to reduce cost and improve health care are:

Reduce administrative cost: The administrative cost of Medicare is currently about 5% of health care expenditures. The administrative cost (including profit) at private insurance companies is about 15%. Insurance companies can continue operating under the proposed Medicare Choice if they add value and control costs, but not if they are only middlemen.

Negotiate fixed prices: A single-payer health care system such as Medicare Choice can negotiate better prices for health care services, products, and drugs. "Fixed prices" can be established in advance so health care providers compete to provide the best service at an affordable price, rather than the best service regardless of price. Of course, fixed prices can vary across the country based on the cost of living.

Establish best practices: Medicare Choice can define "best practices" to standardize health care using the collective wisdom of health care professionals. This ensures that health care resources are expended where they can do the most good and shields doctors from frivolous lawsuits. Most U.S. companies standardize their key processes, so employees know how to do their jobs. Medicare Choice should do the same.

Simplify medical record-keeping: Medicare Choice should use a state-of-the-art, proven database to track patient health care data and pay health care providers. This database can be similar to systems already used in the U.S. and other countries.

Enhance preventive health care: Because Medicare Choice provides cradle-to-grave health care coverage, it offers unique incentives and opportunities to focus on improving public health and preventing health care problems.

Improve financial incentives: Medicare Choice can improve financial incentives so doctors and patients use the health care system wisely and focus on keeping people healthy.

Recent studies indicate that about one-quarter of all U.S. health care expenditures are wasted (Shrank et al, *Waste in the US Health Care System*). By reducing waste, we can improve health care and decrease cost.

Example Financial Incentives to Control Health Care Expenditures

Medicare Choice should use co-pays to encourage wise use of the health care system. For example, it could require a 20% co-pay until a taxpayer's out-of-pocket cost exceeds 20% of income reported on their prior year's tax return. Wellness visits and preventive medicine such as vaccinations should be exempt from this co-pay.

High-income taxpayers should pay the co-pay when they receive health care. However, low-income and middle-income taxpayers should be allowed to delay payment until they prepare their tax returns and deduct it from their refundable tax credit and carbon dividends. This will allow them to receive health care with no out-of-pocket expenses. (This is discussed later, in Chapter 5.6.)

This co-pay is a very important feature of the proposed Medicare Choice. It will decrease cost and improve quality by reducing frivolous and inappropriate use of the system. Since the primary purpose of this co-pay is to encourage wise use of health care, taxpayers should not be allowed to eliminate this incentive by purchasing insurance.

Medicare currently requires 20% co-pays for most medical procedures, just as in the proposed Medicare Choice system. However, these co-pays have not been very effective at controlling Medicare costs in the past because most seniors have reduced or eliminated them by purchasing supplementary insurance or signing up for Medicare Advantage. (Medicare rules are being changed for 2020 and beyond to address this problem.)

Medicare Choice should ensure that all patients are subject to meaningful co-pays. However, taxpayers should be allowed to purchase other types of supplementary insurance (so long as it does not eliminate the 20% co-pay requirement) or opt out. This maximizes freedom of choice and provides funding for the development and testing of alternative health care approaches and advanced medical procedures.

> Readers who want more information on how to control health care costs are encouraged to read the following books:
>
> - *The Healing of America: A Global Quest for Better, Cheaper, and Fairer Health Care* by T. R. Reid
>
> - *The Price We Pay: What Broke American Health Care—and How to Fix It* by Marty Makary

Preventive Health Care Examples

The following examples illustrate how Medicare Choice's cradle-to-grave coverage can improve health care and reduce cost:

Better education, healthier lifestyles, and preventive medicine: In the current health care system, insurance companies have little incentive to improve long-term health, since people frequently transfer from one insurance company to another. Also, people without health care insurance may not get the help they need. As a result, people in the U.S. are not as healthy as they could be. The federal government pays dearly for this when people use Medicaid or turn 65 and become eligible for Medicare. Medicare Choice can improve health care and reduce cost by improving health education, encouraging healthy lifestyles, and providing better preventive health care.

Mental health: The current health care system does not pay sufficient attention to mental health. One reason is that mental health is a long-term issue and insurance companies have little incentive to focus on long-term problems. Homelessness, drug addiction, and gun violence are three of the more obvious consequences of untreated mental health problems. Medicare Choice can improve the treatment of mental health problems.

Health care research and epidemiological studies: The U.S. has fantastic health care research capabilities, but too often, these capabilities are focused on maximizing profits rather than solving the most important health care problems. Medicare Choice can work with other government organizations such as the National Institutes of Health, university researchers, non-profit organizations, and drug companies to focus research where it can do the most good. Researchers will be able to use the Medicare Choice database to perform epidemiological studies to identify problem areas, trends, and potential solutions.

The Veterans Administration (VA) currently operates a health care system for veterans that is totally different from Medicare. In the VA health care system, the government owns the facilities and employs the doctors rather than using private health care providers.

The VA health care system has been a problem for many years. If Medicare Choice is adopted, veterans will no longer need a separate health care system. The VA facilities can be sold to private health care providers. This is a win-win situation. Veterans will receive better health care through Medicare Choice and the VA will no longer have to administer a (failing) health care system. Of course, the military should continue to provide health care on the battlefield and for most active-duty personnel because of their unique needs.

Medicare Choice Should Address the
Unique Needs of Each Age Group

Figure 4-2 shows U.S. health care spending by age group. Medicare already covers age groups with the highest per capita health care costs.

- Age 65–84: $17,000 annual cost per person.

- Over 85: $33,000 annual cost per person.

- For people approaching the end of their life (say, 85 to 90 years old), the primary focus should be on improving the quality of life rather than extending life regardless of cost and pain and suffering.

Younger age groups have lower health care costs.

- For these age groups, the primary focus should be to encourage healthy lifestyles, improve preventive health care, and address health problems proactively.

Figure 4-2. U.S. Health Care Spending by Age Group

**Annual Health Care
Spending (Dollars Per Person)**

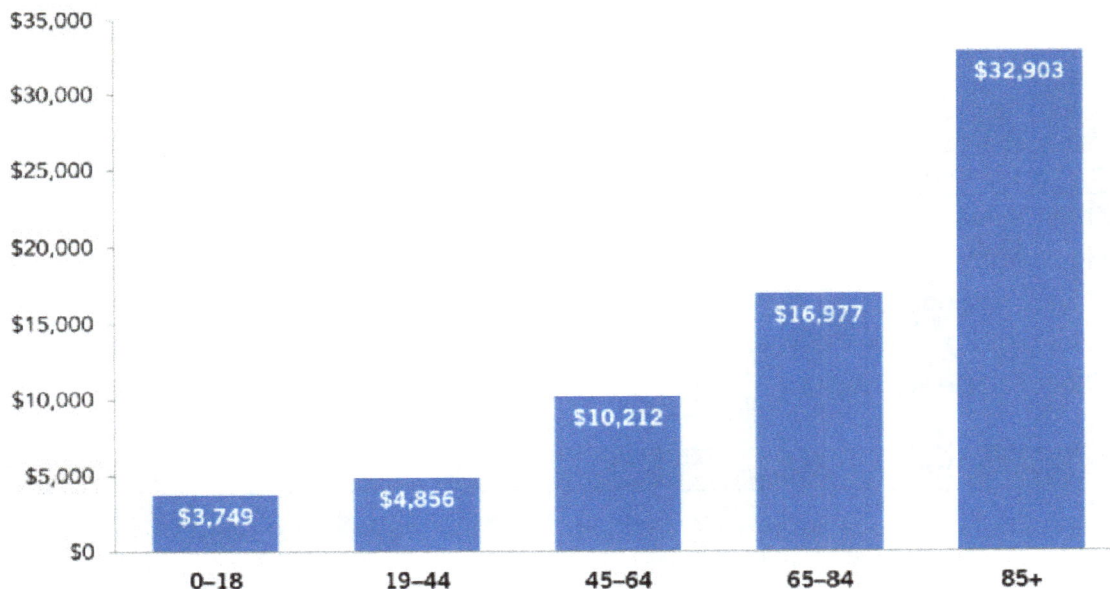

Source: Centers for Medicare and Medicaid Services, *National Health Expenditures by Age and Gender,* April 2019. Data are for 2014. Compiled by the Peter G. Peterson Foundation and used with their permission.

Medicare Choice Cost Allocation

Table 4-1 shows how the proposed Medicare Choice cost target (14% of GDP) might be allocated. The key items to note in this table are:

- The cost of health care in our current system is shown in the second and third columns. The total cost of health care was 17.9% of GDP in 2017 and is projected to increase to 19.4% of GDP by 2027. The federal government currently pays about one-third of the cost of health care. Others (primarily households, private businesses, and state and local governments) pay about two-thirds of the cost.

- The Medicare Choice cost target (14% of GDP) and the proposed allocation of this target to the federal government and other payers is shown in the fourth column. With this allocation, the federal government will pay about two-thirds of the cost of health care, and others will pay about one-third of the cost.

The allocation in the fourth column of Table 4-1 is meant to be a (flexible) guide for the Medicare Choice system rather than rigid (inflexible) objectives. The next page describes the basis for this allocation.

Table 4-1. Medicare Choice Cost Target and Allocation

Payer	Current Health Care Expenditures (% of GDP)		Medicare Choice Cost Target and Allocation (% of GDP)
	2017 (Actuals)	2027 (Projection)	
Federal Government	5.1	6.0	9.0
Other Payers			
- Households	5.0	5.3	3.0
- Private Businesses	3.6	3.7	0.4
- State & Local Governments	3.0	3.2	0.4
- Other Private Revenues	1.2	1.2	1.2
	12.8	13.4	5.0
Total Cost of Health Care	17.9	19.4	14.0

Source: The current health care expenditures in the second and third columns are from the Centers for Medicare and Medicaid Services, *National Health Expenditure Data*. The numbers in the fourth column were developed by the author.

Basis for Medicare Choice Cost Allocation

The cost allocation in Table 4-1 is based on the following considerations:

Federal government (9% of GDP): Medicare Choice will increase federal expenditures for health care. However, the increase will not be as large as some might imagine because the federal government already (1) funds Medicare, (2) pays part of the cost of Medicaid, (3) subsidizes health care insurance for low-income taxpayers (through the Children's Health Insurance Program and the Affordable Care Act), and (4) pays for Veterans and Native American health care. The allocation to the federal government (9% of GDP) is more than federal governments in other developed countries spend for health care. It will nevertheless require Medicare Choice to implement effective cost controls (such as those discussed previously), since the U.S. is starting with a higher-cost health care system.

Households (3% of GDP): Household health care expenses will decrease. Today, most households pay (1) part of the cost of their employer-provided health care plan; (2) co-pays required by their health care plan; (3) Medicare premiums, co-pays, and supplements (for those on Medicare); and (4) out-of-pocket health care expenses. With the proposed Medicare Choice, their primary health care expenditure will be Medicare Choice co-pays. Households will also have miscellaneous out-of-pocket expenses, and those who opt out of Medicare Choice or purchase supplementary insurance may incur additional costs.

Private businesses (0.4% of GDP): Most private businesses currently provide health care insurance for their employees. Their health care expenditures will decrease, since they no longer need to provide this health care insurance. Nevertheless, they will still incur some health care expenses such as workers' compensation insurance, disability insurance, and worksite health care.

State and local governments (0.4% of GDP): State and local governments currently fund health care insurance for their employees and share the cost of Medicaid with the federal government. Their health care expenditures will decrease, since these costs are eliminated. However, they will still incur some health care costs such as public health activities, vocational rehabilitation, and miscellaneous state and local health programs.

Other private revenue (1.2% of GDP): Other private revenue, such as philanthropic support and privately funded facilities, equipment, and research is not expected to change significantly.

Medicare Choice Opt-Out Provision

Many people object to Medicare-for-All because they believe (1) it will decrease personal choice and force people to change doctors and health care plans, and (2) health care could deteriorate due to mismanagement and cost constraints.

To address these concerns, the proposed Medicare Choice allows taxpayers to opt out if they provide health care insurance for themselves and their dependents (either as individuals or as part of a group plan offered by employers or other organizations). In this case, they receive "premium support" equal to the average cost for Medicare Choice to provide for their health care. For example, the premium support might be $3,000 annually for each taxpayer and dependent under 45 years old, $6,000 annually for those between 45 and 65, $10,000 annually for those between 65 and 85, and $20,000 annually for those over 85 years old. Aside from age, the size of the premium support could be adjusted for location and other factors.

To ensure that everyone has health insurance, Medicare Choice should pay the premium support for those who opt out directly to the insurance companies. Taxpayers who select a higher-cost insurance plan will have to pay the additional cost. Medicare Choice will automatically provide health care coverage for all taxpayers and dependents who do not opt out of the system.

This opt-out provision provides two major advantages: (1) it is a "safety relief valve" for those who do not want to transition to Medicare, and (2) it will give Medicare the competition it needs to achieve its full potential.

With this opt-out provision, the proposed Medicare Choice is really a hybrid of two health care systems: Medicare-for-All (favored by many progressive Democrats) and a premium support health care system (favored by many conservative Republicans). This has the potential to receive bipartisan support because it achieves the most important objectives of both Democrats (universal health care) and Republicans (cost control, personal choice, and competition).

Tax Reform Objectives

To design a new tax system, the strategy discussed in the previous 13 pages must be converted into actionable objectives. This is done in Table 4-2. Federal expenditures and tax revenue with the current tax system are shown in the second and third columns; proposed objectives for the new system are shown in the fourth column. See Chapter 5 for how to achieve these objectives. Key items to note here are:

- Health care expenditures are increased to 9.1% of GDP to pay for Medicare Choice. Social Security and discretionary expenditures are also increased slightly.

- Tax revenue is increased by replacing the corporate income tax with a value-added tax. This "tax shift" increases tax revenue by 7.6% of GDP and balances the federal budget.

- The proposed tax reform objectives balance the budget. Federal expenditures and tax revenue are both 25.8% of GDP in this budget.

Table 4-2. Tax Reform Objectives

	Expenditures and Tax Revenue with the Current Tax System		Tax Reform Objectives
Federal Expenditures	2019 (% of GDP)	2025–2029 (% of GDP)	(% of GDP)
Health Care	5.2	6.4	9.1
Social Security	4.9	5.8	6.0
Other Mandatory Programs	2.6	2.4	2.4
Discretionary Expenditures	6.3	5.1	5.5
Net Interest on Debt	1.8	2.9	2.8
Total Expenditures	20.8	22.5	25.8
Federal Tax Revenue			
Individual Income Tax	8.3	9.3	9.3
Payroll Tax	5.8	5.9	6.0
Corporate Income Tax	1.2	1.5	0.0
Value-Added Tax	0.0	0.0	9.1
Other Taxes*	1.3	1.4	1.4
Total Tax Revenue	16.5	18.0	25.8
Deficit or Surplus	-4.3	-4.5	0.0

Source: The expenditures and tax revenue with the current tax system (the second and third columns) are from the Congressional Budget Office, *The Budget and Economic Outlook, 2019 to 2029,* January 2019. The numbers in these two columns do not add due to rounding. The tax reform objectives in the fourth column were developed by the author to fund Medicare Choice, restore Social Security to financial health, increase discretionary expenditures, and balance the budget.

*Includes estate taxes, excise taxes, and other miscellaneous taxes and fees.

The Proposed Tax Reform Does Not Increase the Economic Burden on Taxpayers

Table 4-3 shows why the proposed tax reform does not increase the burden on taxpayers. Key items to note in this table are:

- The taxpayer burden with the current tax system is shown in the second and third columns. Federal tax revenue plus the cost of health care paid by others was 30.1% of GDP in 2017. This is projected to increase to 31.7% of GDP by 2027. If nothing is done to control the cost of health care, the burden on taxpayers will continue increasing after 2027.

- The taxpayer burden with the proposed tax reform is shown in the fourth column. It is 30.8% of GDP. The proposed tax reform increases the cost of health care paid by the federal government but reduces the cost of health care paid by others.

- The proposed tax reform does not increase the total burden on taxpayers. It is slightly over 30% of GDP with the current tax system, and it will remain at a little over 30% of GDP in the new system.

The proposed tax reform strategy balances the federal budget, funds Medicare Choice, restores Social Security to financial health, and increases discretionary spending without increasing the economic burden on taxpayers. How is this possible? The savings achieved by implementing Medicare Choice with cost controls enable all these favorable outcomes.

Table 4-3. Taxpayer Burden Is Not Increased

Expense Category	Taxpayer Burden (% of GDP)		
	Current Tax System		
	2017 (Actuals)	2027 (Projection)	Proposed Tax Reform
Federal Tax Revenue	17.3	18.3	25.8
Cost of Health Care Paid by Others	12.8	13.4	5.0
Total	30.1	31.7	30.8

Source: The federal tax revenue in the second and third columns is from the Congressional Budget Office, *The Budget and Economic Outlook, 2018 to 2028,* April 2018 and *The Budget and Economic Outlook, 2019 to 2029,* January 2019. The federal tax revenue in the third column is from Table 4-2. The cost of health care paid by others is from Table 4-1.

5 BIPARTISAN BALANCED BUDGET (BBB) TAX

The next step in the SE process is to define the new tax system, based on the strategy and objectives described in the previous chapter. The proposed new tax system is named the Bipartisan Balanced Budget (BBB) tax. It includes seven key elements:

Individual income tax: This is a broad-based tax on income. All income is taxed at the same (progressive) rates.

Value-added tax (VAT): This is a flat tax on consumption. Revenue from this tax is earmarked for Medicare Choice.

Payroll tax: This is a flat tax on labor. Revenue from this tax is earmarked for Social Security.

Estate tax: This is a tax on accumulated wealth. Revenue from it is used to improve the education system.

Excise taxes: These are special-purpose taxes levied on certain products and services. A new revenue-neutral "carbon dividends" excise tax is included to address climate change.

Balanced budget feedback mechanism: An automatic feedback mechanism is included to encourage Congress and the president to control spending.

Public disclosure: Candidates for high-level office are required to release their tax returns to increase transparency and promote good governance.

SE Process for Tax Reform

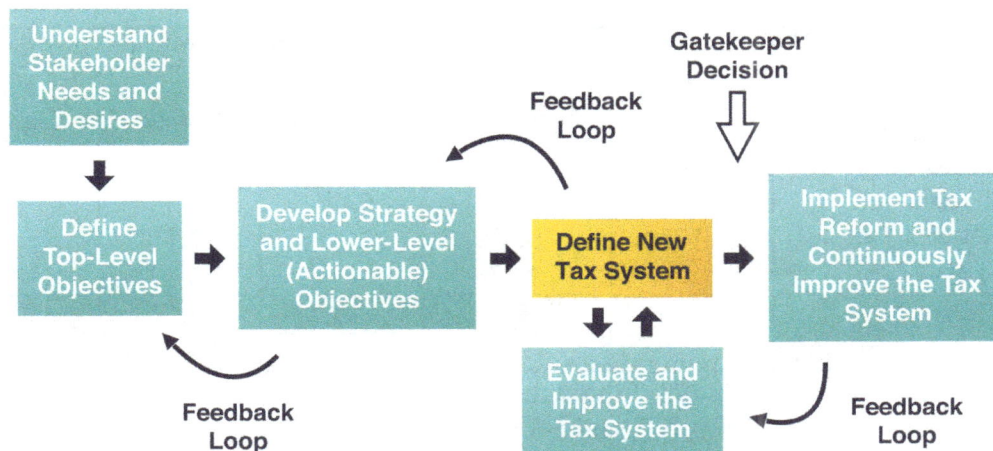

BBB Tax Summary

Table 5-1 summarizes the BBB tax rates, revenue, and expenditures. Key items to note in this table are:

- The BBB tax balances the federal budget. Federal tax revenue and expenditures are both 25.8% of GDP.

- VAT revenue is 9.1% of GDP. It funds Medicare Choice, whose expenditures are also 9.1% of GDP.

- Payroll tax revenue is 6% of GDP. It funds Social Security, whose expenditures are also 6% of GDP.

- The individual income tax (9.3% of GDP) and other taxes (1.4% of GDP) fund all other federal expenditures (10.7% of GDP).

The individual income tax is described in Chapter 5.1. The individual income tax rates (0–36%) are shown in Table 5.1-1 and the income tax revenue (9.3% of GDP) is calculated in Table 5.1-3.

The VAT is described in Chapter 5.2. The VAT tax rate (13%) and revenue (9.1% of GDP) are calculated as shown in Table 5.2-1.

The payroll tax is described in Chapter 5.3. The payroll tax rate (14%) and revenue (6% of GDP) are calculated as shown in Table 5.3-1.

Other taxes include primarily estate taxes (described in Chapter 5.4) and excise taxes (described in Chapter 5.5).

Table 5-1. BBB Tax Summary

Tax	Tax Rate (%)	Tax Revenue (% of GDP)	Expenditures (% of GDP)		
			Social Security	Medicare Choice	All Others
Income Tax	0–36%	9.3%			9.3%
Payroll Tax	14%	6.0%	6.0%		
Value-Added Tax	13%	9.1%		9.1%	
Other Taxes*		1.4%			1.4%
Total		25.8%	6.0%	9.1%	10.7%
			25.8%		

Source: The numbers in columns 3 through 6 are from Table 4-2. The tax rates in column 2 are discussed in Chapter 5.1, 5.2, and 5.3.

* Includes excise taxes, estate and gift taxes, Federal Reserve remittances, customs duties, miscellaneous fees, and fines.

5.1 INDIVIDUAL INCOME TAX

The key principles of the BBB income tax are as follows:

- All income is treated as ordinary income and taxed at the same (progressive) tax rates. The goal is to eliminate tax preferences and not allow any income to escape taxation.

- Itemized deductions and tax credits are eliminated. They are replaced with a (large) standard deduction and a refundable tax credit for each taxpayer and dependent.

These two principles simplify the tax code. Taxable income is calculated simply by adding income from all sources:

- Wages, salaries, tips, and fringe benefits (reported on W-2 form)

- Interest and dividends

- Business income or loss (including self-employment and rental income)

- Capital gains (or losses)

- Pensions, annuities, and IRA distributions

- Social Security benefits

- Other income (such as alimony received, lottery winnings, etc.)

The BBB income tax is calculated using the tax table on the next page. The alternative minimum tax (AMT) is eliminated.

BBB Tax Table

The BBB income tax table is shown in Table 5.1-1. The key differences between this table and the tax table in the current tax code are as follows:

- The standard deduction is increased from $12,000 to $15,000 for single taxpayers and from $24,000 to $30,000 for married couples filing jointly. All itemized deductions are eliminated.

- Each taxpayer and dependent receives a (new) $1,000 refundable tax credit. All other tax credits are eliminated. This refundable tax credit is designed to offset the loss of other tax credits, especially the earned income tax credit (EITC) and the child tax credits in the current tax code.

- The number of tax rates is reduced from six in the current tax code (12%, 22%, 24%, 32%, 35%, and 37%) to four (10%, 20%, 28%, and 36%).

- The three top tax brackets are adjusted downward to approximately "cancel out" the standard deduction and refundable tax credit for high-income taxpayers. This is a better approach than using complex rules to "phase out" the standard deduction and refundable tax credit.

The standard deduction, refundable tax credit, and tax brackets are all indexed for inflation.

Table 5.1-1. Individual Income Tax Rates and Tax Brackets

Tax Rate	Single Taxpayers	Married Filing Jointly	Head of Household
0% (Standard Deduction)	<$15,000	<$30,000	<$21,000
10%	$15,000–$40,000	$30,000–$80,000	$21,000–$56,000
20%	$40,000–$90,000	$80,000–$180,000	$56,000–$126,000
28%	$90,000–$150,000	$180,000–$300,000	$126,000–$210,000
36%	>$150,000	>$300,000	>$210,000

Source: The numbers in this table were developed by the author. In addition to the tax brackets and tax rates shown here, each taxpayer and dependent receives a refundable $1,000 tax credit.

Individual Income Tax Example
for Representative Taxpayers

Table 5.1-2 shows the individual income tax owed by 15 representative taxpayers. The most important items to notice in this table are:

Low-income taxpayers (white cells) pay no income tax and receive a refundable tax credit. Their average income tax rate is negative. The low-income taxpayers in this example receive $500 to $3,000 from the IRS each year (the numbers in parentheses).

Middle-income taxpayers (dark orange cells) pay some income tax, but only a little. Their average income tax rate, shown in the far-right column, is 1% to 4%.

High-income and very-high-income taxpayers (light orange cells) in this example pay an average income tax rate of 13% to 26%.

Although not shown on this table, taxpayers with very high income (say, over $1 million annually) will pay an average income tax rate of 30% to 36%.

Table 5.1-2. Income Tax for Representative Taxpayers

Taxpayer Filing Status	Taxable Income ($)	Tax from Tax Table ($)	Refundable Tax Credit ($)	Tax After Tax Credit ($)	Average Tax Rate (%)
Married Filing Jointly with Two Dependents	40,000	1,000	4,000	(3,000)	-8%
	80,000	5,000	4,000	1,000	1%
	200,000	30,600	4,000	26,600	13%
	500,000	130,600	4,000	126,600	25%
Single	20,000	500	1,000	(500)	-3%
	40,000	2,500	1,000	1,500	4%
	100,000	15,300	1,000	14,300	14%
	250,000	65,300	1,000	64,300	26%
Head of Household with One Dependent	28,000	700	2,000	(1,300)	-5%
	56,000	3,500	2,000	1,500	3%
	140,000	21,420	2,000	19,420	14%
	350,000	91,420	2,000	89,420	26%

Source: The numbers in this table were calculated by the author using the tax brackets and tax rates in Table 5.1-1.

Estimated Individual Income Tax Revenue
for 2025–2029

Table 5.1-3 provides the estimated revenue from the BBB income tax. The key items to note on this table are:

- The BBB income tax is progressive. The top 1% of taxpayers pay almost half of all income tax. The next 9% pay one-third of all income taxes and the bottom 50% pay no income tax.

- Income tax revenue is 10.1% of GDP before the refundable tax credit and 8.6% of GDP after the refundable tax credit. The difference between these two numbers is the refundable tax credit (1.5% of GDP).

- Part of the refundable tax credit (0.8% of GDP) will reduce the tax owed by high-income and middle-income taxpayers, and the remainder (0.7% of GDP) is refunded to low-income taxpayers. The refunded amount is included as a budget item under "mandatory payments." The net income tax collected is 9.3% of GDP.

The BBB income tax is slightly more progressive than the current income tax. However, since the BBB tax includes (flat) VAT and payroll taxes, most taxpayers pay some tax. This is discussed in more detail in Chapter 5.9.

Table 5.1-3. Revenue Estimate for BBB Individual Income Tax

Taxpayer Category	Taxable Income (% of GDP)	Average Income Tax Rate (%)		Income Tax Revenue (% of GDP)	
		Before Refundable Tax Credit	After Refundable Tax Credit	Before Refundable Tax Credit	After Refundable Tax Credit
Top 1%	14%	30.0%	29.9%	4.2%	4.2%
Top 1–10%	17%	19.0%	18.0%	3.2%	3.1%
Top 10–50%	26%	9.5%	7.0%	2.5%	1.8%
Bottom 50%	8%	2.0%	-6.0%	0.2%	-0.5%
	65%			10.1%	8.6%
Total Refundable Tax Credit (10.1% - 8.6%) =				1.5% of GDP	
Refundable Tax Credit Used to Reduce Tax =				0.8% of GDP	
Refundable Tax Credit Refunded as Cash =				0.7% of GDP	
Net Income Tax Rate (10.1% - 0.8%) =				9.3% of GDP	

Source: The numbers in this table were estimated by the author using the BBB tax table (Table 5.1-1) and IRS data from 2017 income tax returns.

Why Eliminate Itemized Deductions and Tax Credits?

Engineers strive for simplicity. They often use the term "KISS" to express this aim. It means "keep it simple and smart" or "keep it simple, stupid." Engineers know from experience that unnecessarily complex products are difficult to design, build, operate, and maintain.

Simplicity is as important for the tax system as for engineered products. A complex tax system is difficult to design, implement, use, and maintain.

The current tax system includes hundreds of itemized deductions and tax credits. Some deductions and credits are simple, but many have complex rules for who qualifies and how the rules are phased out for high-income taxpayers. Each deduction and credit may appear reasonable if viewed in isolation, but together, they make the tax code unnecessarily complex.

Besides complexity, itemized deductions and tax credits cause several other problems:

- They corrupt the political process because special interests frequently try to "buy" favorable deductions and credits by contributing to politicians who support them.

- They cause other tax rates to increase (to offset revenue loss due to itemized deductions and tax credits).

- They can have unintended consequences and may cause taxpayers to make poor decisions just to avoid taxes. For example, the cost of housing has skyrocketed partly because the current tax code allows homeowners to deduct mortgage interest and property taxes (up to a limit) and pay no tax on capital gains (up to a limit). These tax preferences were enacted to help taxpayers afford home ownership, but they have also increased the price of homes and priced some people out of the market for home ownership.

It is politically impractical to eliminate most itemized deductions and tax credits without eliminating them all. So, the BBB tax eliminates all itemized deductions and tax credits; it replaces them with a large standard deduction and a $1,000 refundable tax credit for each taxpayer and dependent.

The current tax system phases out many deductions and tax credits for wealthy taxpayers. This adds complexity to the tax code. The BBB tax does not phase out its standard deduction and refundable tax credit. However, it achieves the same effect in a much simpler way by lowering the tax brackets for high-income taxpayers. The tax brackets in Table 5.1-1 were chosen to achieve this.

Capital Gains and Dividends
Are Taxed as Ordinary Income

Capital gains and dividends are taxed at the same rate as income from other sources. This is appropriate since the BBB tax eliminates the corporate income tax. It is simpler, fairer, and more efficient to tax corporate income as part of two broad-based taxes (the VAT and the individual income tax) rather than as a separate corporate income tax with special rules for capital gains and dividends.

Capital gains still receive favorable tax treatment, since they are not taxed until an asset is sold. This is justifiable as it roughly offsets the effect of inflation.

The BBB tax eliminates tax loopholes associated with capital gains:

- No like-kind exchanges of real estate and other assets. Capital gains taxes are due when an asset is sold.

- No forgiveness of capital gains when an asset is given to a non-profit organization or charity.

- No step-up in value when the owner of an asset passes away. Whoever inherits the asset pays the capital gains tax when it is sold. If an asset is sold by an estate, the estate pays the capital gains tax.

The BBB tax eliminates the capital gains exemption on the sale of a primary residence ($250,000 for single taxpayers and $500,000 for married taxpayers filing jointly). To avoid spiking income too much in one year, homeowners may spread the capital gain equally over five years.

- This allows low-income and middle-income taxpayers to move up to better homes and (if necessary) sell their homes to fund retirement.

- Wealthy taxpayers cannot avoid taxes by purchasing and selling multiple high-cost homes.

- These changes should slow the rapid appreciation of house prices in "hot" markets, which is pricing many people out of home ownership.

Pensions, Retirement Accounts, and
Social Security Benefits Are Taxed as Ordinary Income

The following provisions of the current tax system are not changed:

- Employer and employee contributions to pension plans are tax-deferred. Pension income is taxed when received.

- Employer and employee contributions to retirement accounts (e.g., 401k plans) are tax-deferred. Distributions are taxed when received (like pensions).

- Pension plans and retirement accounts grow tax-free (like capital gains).

The following provisions of the current tax code are changed:

- Social Security income is taxed at the same rate as other sources of income.

- Roth IRA plans are eliminated, since they allow income to escape taxation. Current Roth IRA accounts are phased out as follows: no more contributions are allowed, and they are closed and liquidated when the owner passes away.

Fringe Benefit Tax Loophole Is Eliminated

Many fringe benefits escape taxation in the current tax code. For example, employer-provided health care insurance is excluded from taxation. It is not taxed under the (1) income tax, (2) payroll tax, or (3) corporate income tax. This triple exclusion (or loophole) reduced federal tax revenue by $340 billion in 2017.

The BBB tax eliminates the fringe benefit loophole in two ways.

First, the value-added tax inherently taxes fringe benefits, just as it does corporate profits. This is a significant advantage of the value-added tax. It is an elegantly simple way to ensure that fringe benefits and other untaxed and underreported incomes do not escape taxation.

Second, the BBB tax reduces the fringe benefit exclusions to the following:

- **Pension and retirement contributions:** The tax on these fringe benefits is deferred until the taxpayer receives the pension or withdraws money from a retirement account. This deferral is justified because (1) it defers but does not eliminate taxes, just like the treatment of capital gains; and (2) there is no other practical way to tax defined benefit retirement plans.

- **Working condition benefits:** This exclusion is limited to property and services a company provides so an employee can perform his or her job. This includes items such as work-related travel expenses, vehicles, uniforms, and safety equipment. It also includes items such as on-site meals, day care facilities, and education assistance, if they are provided primarily to improve employee performance.

- **De minimus (minimal) benefits:** Small fringe benefits with little monetary value or cost are excluded because the expense of bookkeeping far exceeds the value of collecting taxes on these items.

Some employers may want to pay the income tax on taxable fringe benefits rather than burdening employees with this responsibility. They should be allowed to do this. However, since employees are in different income tax brackets, employers would have to pay the highest income tax rate in the tax table (36%).

Interest Income Is Taxed as Ordinary Income

Interest income is taxed at the same rate as income from other sources. This differs from the current tax code, which taxes interest at various rates.

Tax-free bonds issued by cities, schools, and other public entities are eliminated. This eliminates a significant tax loophole and ensures that all sources of income are taxed at the same (progressive) rates.

This can be implemented as follows: existing bonds remain tax-free, but after a transition period, no new tax-free bonds are allowed.

As a result of this change, cities, schools, and other public entities that currently use tax-free bonds will pay higher interest rates. This increased cost will be partially offset by their reduced cost for employee health care. Nevertheless, the higher interest cost will encourage them to "pay as you go" and issue fewer bonds.

5.2 VALUE-ADDED TAX—HEALTH CARE

The BBB tax eliminates the 21% corporate income tax and replaces it with a 13% value-added tax (VAT). VAT revenue is earmarked to fund Medicare Choice.

The proposed VAT is a broad-based flat tax levied on businesses, non-profit organizations, and federal, state, and local governments based on their value-added. It is calculated as follows:

- Businesses calculate their VAT with the "credit-invoice" method. This means they pay the VAT on their total sales and receive a credit for VAT included on the invoices for their purchases from other businesses.

- Non-profit organizations and federal, state, and local governments that do not sell products cannot use the credit-invoice method to calculate their VAT. Instead, they calculate their value-added directly, by adding their cost for labor, fringe benefits, rent, and interest.

Table 5.2-1 shows the revenue available to fund Medicare Choice. The VAT revenue (9.1% of GDP) is calculated by multiplying the fraction of GDP taxed by the VAT (0.7) times the VAT tax rate (13%). The fraction of GDP taxed by the VAT (0.7) is based on an analysis by the Urban-Brookings Tax Policy Center, which shows that a broad-based VAT can tax 70% of GDP, even after allowing for noncompliance and a small business exemption.

The broad-based VAT proposed here is appropriate since it funds Medicare Choice, which relieves businesses, non-profit organizations, and federal, state, and local governments of the need to fund their employees' health care.

Even though this VAT is a flat tax, it is progressive since it funds Medicare Choice. It is also a "wealth tax" since taxpayers who have accumulated a lot of wealth will eventually pay the VAT when they or their heirs "spend down" their assets.

Table 5.2-1. Value-Added Tax (VAT) Revenue

Fraction of GDP taxed by the VAT =	0.7 (70%)
VAT tax rate =	13%
VAT revenue =	9.1% of GDP (0.7 x 13%)

Source: The fraction of GDP taxed by the VAT (70%) is based on the Tax Policy Center report *Using the VAT to Reform the Income Tax,* January 2012. The VAT tax rate (13%) is set to achieve the revenue needed to fund Medicare Choice.

VAT Advantages

The VAT proposed here has many advantages. Three of the most important are:

- **Medicare Choice:** The VAT is the best way to fund Medicare Choice. All other developed countries have both a VAT and universal health care. Without a VAT, they would not have sufficient tax revenue to fund universal health care. Although it is possible to fund universal health care without a VAT, there is no precedent for doing so anywhere in the world. To fund Medicare Choice without a VAT (say, by significantly increasing individual and corporate income tax rates) would involve a considerable risk of increased tax avoidance and evasion. So, based on experience in other countries, the VAT is the most practical and lowest risk approach to fund Medicare Choice.

- **Economic growth:** The VAT will make U.S. companies more competitive and stimulate sustainable economic growth for four reasons. First, because the VAT funds Medicare Choice, it will eliminate the competitive disadvantage that U.S. companies currently face when competing against companies in countries with lower-cost, government-funded health care. Second, because the VAT replaces the corporate income tax, it will give U.S. companies a competitive advantage over companies in other countries with a corporate income tax. Third, the VAT will level the playing field in the global marketplace, since importers must pay the VAT for imports, and exporters receive a VAT credit for exports. Fourth, because the VAT taxes consumption, it will encourage savings and investment. Increased savings and investment will promote healthy, sustainable, long-term economic growth.

- **More and better jobs:** As U.S. businesses become more competitive and expand production, they will create jobs. The jobs created will often command higher salaries and wages, since businesses no longer need to fund their employees' health care. This effect will be most noticeable for low-income and moderate-income employees whose health care costs are large compared to their salaries. For example, a company that currently pays an employee $30,000 annually and spends $20,000 for health care for the employee and their family may be willing to pay that employee $40,000 or more when they no longer need to provide health care. The VAT should spur a significant increase in the minimum wage to ensure that businesses share the benefits of their new-found competitiveness with their employees.

A key argument against a VAT is that it will decrease consumer spending. This is a significant concern since consumer spending is an important driver of economic growth. However, the tax reform proposed here will maintain strong consumer spending by stimulating economic growth, creating more jobs, and increasing disposable income, especially for low-income and moderate-income taxpayers.

5.3 PAYROLL TAX—SOCIAL SECURITY

The BBB tax restores Social Security to financial health as follows:

- The Social Security payroll tax is increased from 12.4% of GDP to 14% of GDP. Employers and employees each pay half of the payroll tax, as in the current tax code.

- The wage cap on taxable income is eliminated. Fringe benefit exclusions are also reduced as discussed in Chapter 5.1.

- All payroll taxes are earmarked for Social Security. The current 2.9% Medicare payroll tax is eliminated, since VAT funds Medicare Choice. As a result, the overall payroll tax rate is reduced from 15.4% to 14%.

- Social Security benefits are taxed as ordinary income.

All new state and local government employees are required to join Social Security. This provision is included to simplify Social Security and get states and local governments out of the (financially hazardous) business of funding employee pensions.

Table 5.3-1 shows the revenue and assets available to fund Social Security benefits. The key items to note in this table are:

- Payroll tax revenue is 6% of GDP. This is calculated by multiplying the fraction of GDP that is labor income (0.43) times the payroll tax rate (14%).

- The Social Security Trust Fund is currently $2.9 trillion. The goal of the proposed tax reform is to maintain a sizable trust fund to protect Social Security against future economic shocks and unforeseen circumstances.

Table 5.3-1. Payroll Tax Revenue

Fraction of GDP taxed as labor income	0.43
Payroll tax rate	14%
Payroll tax revenue	6% of GDP (0.43 x 14%)
Social Security Trust Fund	$2.9 trillion

Source: The fraction of GDP taxed as labor income (0.43) is based on data from the Congressional Budget Office. The payroll tax rate (14%) is set to achieve the revenue needed to fully fund Social Security. The Social Security Trust Fund ($2.9 trillion) is based on data from the Social Security Administration.

5.4 ESTATE AND GIFT TAXES

The BBB estate and gift taxes are similar to current estate and gift taxes, except that the exemption is reduced to $6 million, and revenue from the estate tax is earmarked for an Education Trust Fund. The key features of the BBB estate and gift taxes are:

- Estates pay no tax on funds given to a spouse or non-profit organization. They pay a tax of 40% on other assets over $6 million. A taxpayer who does not use the full $6 million exemption may transfer it to a spouse. The $6 million exemption is indexed for inflation.

- The estate tax should generate revenue of about $20 billion to $40 billion annually, or 0.1% to 0.2% of GDP. This is much less than the U.S. currently spends for education (about 5% of GDP). Nevertheless, if used effectively, it could significantly improve the education system. To achieve this objective, estate tax revenue is deposited into an Education Trust Fund, which is described on the next page.

- Gifts to spouses and non-profit organizations are not taxed. Gifts to others are taxed only if they exceed $15,000 per person per year and their cumulative value exceeds the $6 million lifetime estate tax exemption. The gift tax rate is 40%, the same as the estate tax rate.

Some people denigrate the estate tax by calling it a death tax, but it is actually a wealth tax. What better way to tax wealth than after a taxpayer has passed away? By using it to improve education, it will create better job opportunities for low-income and middle-income taxpayers and make U.S. companies more competitive. This is fair. It is not unreasonable to ask wealthy taxpayers to give back to society, especially after they and their spouse have passed away. If they want to avoid the estate tax, they can donate their wealth to non-profit organizations of their choice, either while they are alive or in their wills.

In addition to estate taxes, estates must also pay the following: (1) income taxes and Medicare Choice co-pays owed by the deceased at the time of death; and (2) income tax on any income earned by the estate, including capital gains on assets sold by the estate.

As with the current tax system, income earned by an estate can be either (1) taxed at the top rate in the individual income tax table (36%), or (2) distributed to the heirs and added to their income for tax purposes.

Why Create an Education Trust Fund?

The U.S. currently spends about 5% of GDP on education, or about $1 trillion annually. Most of this money is spent by state and local governments. Other developed countries also spend about 5% of their GDP for education.

The objective of the Education Trust Fund is to improve the U.S. education system, especially for students from low-income and middle-income families, without significantly increasing the cost of education (as a percentage of GDP). It will achieve this objective by funding or cost-sharing pilot projects to test various methods to improve the education system.

All interested organizations should be encouraged to propose pilot projects: individual schools, school districts, states, private and non-profit schools, private industry, and non-profit organizations. Typically, pilot projects should have a duration of several years, but the impact on the students involved should be tracked long enough to determine their cost-effectiveness. Each organization that performs a pilot project should document the results with support from trust fund personnel.

The trust fund should prepare an annual report summarizing the pilot projects funded by them and the most important conclusions, lessons learned, and best practices. Local school boards, states, and private schools should then be encouraged (but not required) to use the results to improve their schools and programs. The pilot projects funded by the Education Trust Fund might focus on the following objectives:

Pre-school education: Studies have shown that pre-school education is important to establish a solid foundation for learning. Pilot projects might focus on how to maximize the benefit of pre-school and how best to fund pre-school for all.

K-12 education: Although there are many ideas about how to improve primary and secondary education, there is a lack of good data about which methods are most cost-effective. Pilot projects could provide the data needed by schools and parents to make wise choices to achieve the best education at the lowest cost.

College: Pilot studies might focus on how to reduce the cost of college, motivate students to learn more and waste less time during college, and increase completion rates.

Career and technical education: The education system should prepare students to enter the work force, whether or not they finish high school or college. Pilot projects could assess how career and technical education can best be integrated into high school and college curriculums, and how vocational schools and apprenticeship programs can be improved and made more attractive to students.

5.5 EXCISE TAXES

The current tax code uses excise taxes mainly to achieve two objectives:

- **Objective #1:** Fund infrastructure and services. For example, the excise tax on motor vehicle fuels funds highways and mass transit systems. The excise tax on airline tickets funds airports and air traffic control.

- **Objective #2:** Discourage harmful products and activities and reimburse society for the cost of harm caused by them. For example, the tax on cigarettes discourages smoking and reimburses society for the added health care costs for cigarette smokers.

The BBB tax embraces and strengthens these objectives by making the following two changes to the current tax code.

Highway Trust Fund: Federal motor vehicle fuel taxes are currently 18.4 cents per gallon for gasoline and 24.4 cents per gallon for diesel fuel. These tax rates have not changed since 1993 and are not indexed to inflation. The tax revenue they provide is insufficient to maintain and improve the transportation infrastructure. Therefore, Congress and the president periodically provide extra funding from general tax revenue. To fix this problem permanently, the Highway Trust Fund is renamed the Transportation Trust Fund, with two sub-funds: a Highway Trust Fund and a Mass Transit Trust Fund. These trust funds would be funded as follows:

- Motor vehicle fuel taxes (about $40 billion annually) are indexed for inflation, and all revenue from them is earmarked for the Highway Trust Fund.

- Two percent of income tax revenue (about $40 billion annually) is transferred to the Transportation Trust Fund each year. Half is deposited into the Highway Trust Fund and the other half is deposited into the Mass Transit Trust Fund.

Investing in the transportation infrastructure is important because it provides good jobs, stimulates private investment (to take advantage of the improved transportation infrastructure), and provides a solid foundation for future economic growth. Since all Americans benefit from investments in the transportation infrastructure, it is appropriate to fund them with a combination of motor vehicle fuel taxes and income taxes.

Carbon dividends: The BBB tax includes carbon dividends, a new revenue-neutral excise tax. They are described in the next chapter.

5.6 CARBON DIVIDENDS

Carbon dividends are included in the BBB tax primarily to address climate change. However, they provide other important side benefits, especially when implemented as part of comprehensive tax reform. The key features of carbon dividends are:

- **Carbon fee:** A gradually increasing carbon fee is collected from fossil fuel companies. This fee is levied on oil, natural gas, and coal companies at the wellhead, mine, or port of entry.

- **Carbon dividends:** All fees collected are returned to the American people with quarterly or monthly carbon dividend checks.

- **Border adjustment:** Importers of carbon-intensive products pay a fee (and exporters receive a credit) to ensure a level playing field for American companies and workers.

- **Regulations:** Government regulations that are no longer necessary to address climate change are phased out.

Carbon-intensive products receive border adjustments for two reasons. First, this will ensure that manufacturing does not move abroad just to avoid the carbon fee. Second, border adjustments will trigger a global "domino effect" as other countries scramble to price carbon to avoid (legal) tariffs on their products. This will rapidly reduce global greenhouse gas emissions.

> "All taxes discourage something. Why not discourage bad things like pollution rather than good things like working and investment."
>
> — Lawrence Summers
>
> "As we peer into the future, we—you and I, and our government—must avoid the impulse to live only for today, plundering for our own ease and convenience the precious resources of tomorrow."
>
> — Dwight Eisenhower

Carbon Dividends Example
(Note: All currency values are in constant 2019 dollars.)

The following example illustrates how carbon dividends might work in actual practice. In this example, the carbon fee starts at $20 per ton of carbon dioxide and increases $10 per ton annually for 18 years, until it is $200 per ton. Then:

- The carbon dividends will be roughly $500 annually per person in the second year (or $2,000 for a family of four) and grow to about $1,500 annually per person after 18 years (or $6,000 for a family of four).

- The carbon fee will add 20 cents to the price of a gallon of gasoline initially and $2.00 per gallon after 18 years. The price of other products and services will also increase, depending on how much energy is consumed in their production.

- For most Americans, the carbon dividends will be as large or larger than the extra cost they pay for energy and other products and services.

- Companies will be incentivized to develop clean energy technologies and more efficient products and processes. This will stimulate economic growth and reduce air pollution.

U.S. greenhouse gas emissions were 6.5 billion tons in 2016. A carbon dividend bill might initially cover only 6 billion tons. So, two years after enactment, the carbon dividend might be roughly $500 per person per year (6 billion tons x $30 per ton / 340 million people).

The carbon dividend will increase each year as the carbon fee increases. For example: in 18 years, if the carbon fee is $200 per ton and greenhouse gas emissions are reduced to 3 billion tons, the carbon dividend will be slightly over $1,500 per person per year (3 billion tons x $200 per ton / 380 million people).

Eventually, the carbon dividend will decrease as greenhouse gas emissions are reduced further. For example: in 40 years, if the carbon fee is $300 per ton and greenhouse gas emissions are 1 billion tons, the carbon dividend will be roughly $750 per person per year (1 billion tons x $300 per ton / 410 million people).

After 40 years, the carbon dividend may stabilize, perhaps in the range of $500 to $1,000 per person per year, when the U.S. is carbon neutral and human-caused emissions are equal to natural carbon sinks.

Carbon Dividends Provide Many Benefits

Carbon dividends will decrease greenhouse gas emissions and air pollution without damaging the economy. An analysis by REMI (Regional Economic Models, Inc.) calculates these benefits:

- **Lower carbon dioxide emissions:** 33% reduction in 10 years; 50% lower in 20 years

- **Less air pollution:** 80,000 lives saved over 10 years; 230,000 lives saved over 20 years

- **More jobs:** 2.1 million more jobs in 10 years; 2.8 million more jobs in 20 years

- **Faster economic growth:** $70 billion higher GDP and $500 higher per capita income in 10 years

Other studies show similar results. All studies to date indicate that carbon dividends will reduce carbon dioxide emissions and air pollution. No studies suggest carbon dividends will substantially damage the economy.

Economic analyses are uncertain. Nevertheless, they suggest that carbon dividends may improve the economy, or at least not damage it.

Carbon dividends encourage companies to develop clean energy technologies and more efficient products. They also create a vibrant market for these clean and efficient technologies and products.

Carbon dividends will also reduce income inequality. A study by the U.S. Treasury Department (Horowitz et al.) shows that if carbon dividends are distributed equally to all Americans, then:

- The poorest one-tenth of Americans will see their disposable incomes increase about 10%.

- Low-income and middle-income taxpayers (70% of Americans) will have higher disposable incomes.

- The richest one-tenth of Americans will see their disposable incomes decrease by about 1%.

Carbon Dividends Are Similar to the Popular Alaska Permanent Fund

Alaska taxes oil companies and deposits the tax revenue into the Alaska Permanent Fund. Alaska residents receive annual dividends paid from this fund. The size of the dividends has varied from year to year, as shown in Figure 5.6-1. For the past 37 years they have averaged $1,157 per person.

Alaskans love their annual dividend payments. U.S. taxpayers will probably like carbon dividends as much as Alaskans love their Permanent Fund dividends.

Figure 5.6-1. Alaska Permanent Fund Annual Dividends

Annual Dividend (per person)

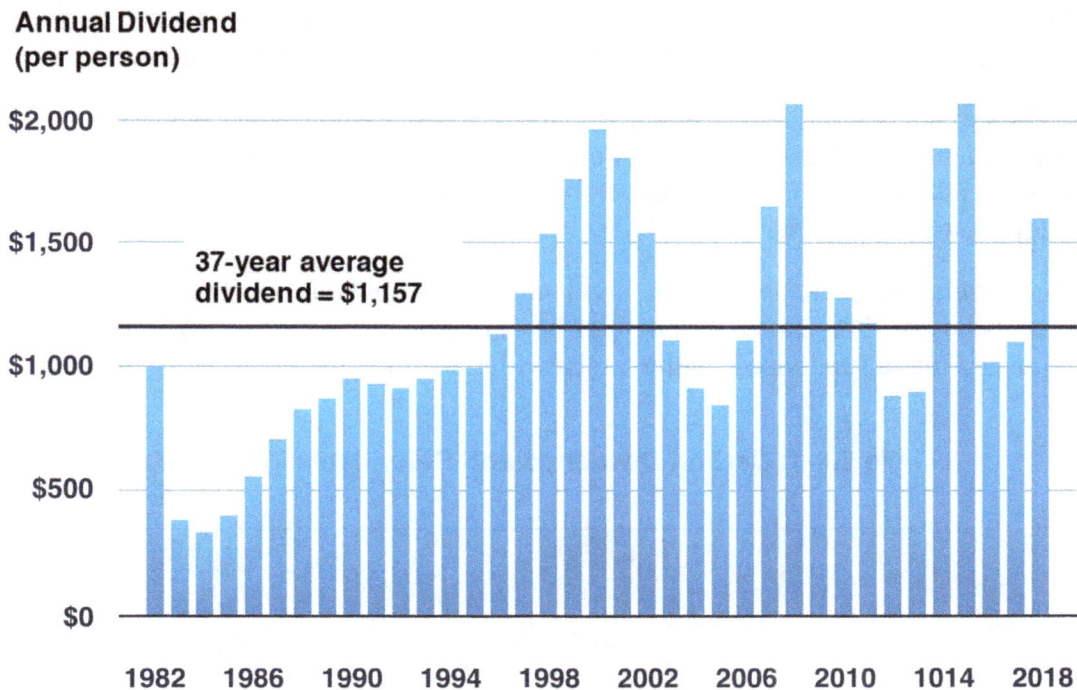

Source: Alaska Permanent Fund Corporation, *Annual Dividend Payouts.* Compiled by the author.

Carbon Dividends and Refundable Tax Credits
Are Important Features of the BBB Tax

Table 5.6-1 shows the annual carbon dividends and refundable tax credits for a single taxpayer, a married couple with no children, and a married couple with two children. The key item to note on this table is the bottom line: (1) single taxpayers receive $1,500 to $2,500 annually from the carbon dividend and tax credit, (2) married couples with no dependents receive $3,000 to $5,000 annually, and (3) married couples with two dependents receive $6,000 to $10,000 annually. These cash payments, which will increase with inflation, provide many advantages. Four of the most important are:

- They provide valuable income support for low-income and middle-income taxpayers. This, coupled with a strong safety net anchored by Medicare Choice and Social Security, will help them move up the income ladder.

- Taxpayers must file tax returns to receive their carbon dividends and tax credits. This will encourage everyone to file tax returns, whether or not they owe taxes.

- Carbon dividends and refundable tax credits provide a simple and effective way for the government to collect unpaid fees. For example, unpaid Medicare Choice co-pays and unpaid child support can be deducted from carbon dividends and refundable tax credits before distributing them.

- The government can use carbon dividends and refundable tax credits to encourage good behavior. For example, they can be (1) denied to anyone who is in jail, or (2) deposited into a supervised fund to assist with rehabilitation and re-entry into society.

Table 5.6-1. Carbon Dividends and Refundable Tax Credits

Source of Funds	Value ($ per Person per Year)	Single Taxpayer	Married Couple	
			No Dependents	Two Dependents
Carbon Dividends	$500–$1,500	$500–$1,500	$1,000–$3,000	$2,000–$6,000
Tax Credit	$1,000	$1,000	$2,000	$4,000
Total		$1,500–$2,500	$3,000–$5,000	$6,000–$10,000

Source: The numbers in this table were developed by the author based on the BBB tax refundable tax credit ($1,000 per person) and the carbon dividend after two years.

Many Companies and Organizations
Support Carbon Dividends

Two major organizations have been formed specifically to promote carbon dividends: the Citizens' Climate Lobby and the Climate Leadership Council.

The Citizens' Climate Lobby is an international organization with more than 100,000 members promoting carbon dividends in the U.S. and throughout the world. It is a bipartisan organization, but it is left-of-center because significantly more than half of its members are Democrats.

The Climate Leadership Council was formed by prominent Republicans to promote carbon dividends. Even though this is a Republican organization, some of its founding members are Democrats. The following people, companies, and organizations are the founding members of the Climate Leadership Council:

- Seventeen respected elder statesmen and opinion leaders (George Schultz; James Baker, III; Janet Yellen; Ben Bernanke; Lawrence Summers; Steven Chu; Stephen Hawking; Greg Mankiw; Ted Halstead; Martin Feldstein; Ray Dalio; Christine Todd Whitman; Ratan Tata; Rob Walton; Paul Polman; Klaus Schwab; and Tom Stephenson)

- Five oil and gas companies: ExxonMobil, BP, Shell, ConocoPhillips, and Total

- Two automobile manufacturers: GM and Ford

- An electric utility: Exelon

- A telecommunications company: AT&T

- Three consumer products companies: P&G, PepsiCo, and Unilever

- Two insurance companies: Allianz and Metlife

- A solar energy company: First Solar

- A health care company: Johnson & Johnson

- A technology company: Microsoft

- The largest engineering firm in the world: AECOM

- Four major environmental organizations (World Wildlife Fund, The Nature Conservancy, World Resources Institute, and Conservation International)

The Climate Leadership Council has formed two other organizations to promote carbon dividends: Americans for Carbon Dividends and Students for Carbon Dividends.

Americans Support Carbon Dividends
by a 2-to-1 Margin

Carbon dividends have broad bipartisan support. A recent public opinion survey shows that Republicans, Democrats, and Independents all support carbon dividends by at least a 2-to-1 margin.

Survey question: "As you may know, some Republican party leaders have proposed requiring fossil fuel companies (coal, oil, and natural gas) to pay a tax on their carbon emissions and rebating all the money collected directly to all Americans through a monthly check. This proposed policy is called carbon dividends because all households would receive a monthly cash dividend as part of an effort to combat climate change. Do you support or oppose this plan?"

Survey results: 58% favor, 23% oppose

- Republicans: 62% favor, 20% oppose

- Democrats: 55% favor, 23% oppose

- Independents: 49% favor, 24% oppose

Voters favor direct cash rebates over all other uses of carbon tax revenue. The survey found that voters prefer cash dividends over the following alternatives: (1) promoting renewable energy, (2) paying down the national debt, (3) infrastructure improvements, (4) reducing income taxes or payroll taxes, (5) assisting low-income communities, (6) climate adaptation, and (7) reducing the corporate income tax.

Survey details: These results are based on an online survey of 1,876 registered voters in August 2018. This survey was conducted by Nexus Polling for the Yale Program on Climate Change Communication and George Mason University Center for Climate Change Communication.

Over 40 countries have adopted carbon taxes or carbon dividends. The countries with the highest carbon taxes in 2018 were Sweden, Switzerland, Finland, and Norway, with carbon taxes of $50 to $130 per ton of carbon dioxide.

The carbon fee proposed here would start much smaller (about $20 per ton of carbon dioxide) and grow slowly to encourage a gradual shift from fossil fuels to clean and renewable energy and development of more energy-efficient products and processes.

Leading Economists and Elder Statesmen
Support Carbon Dividends

The *Wall Street Journal* printed the following statement in January 2019. It was signed by four former Federal Reserve leaders, 15 former chairpersons of the president's Council of Economic Advisors, and 27 Nobel Prize-winning economists. Their statement is as follows:

"Global climate change is a serious problem calling for immediate national action. Guided by sound economic principles, we are united in the following policy recommendations.

I. A carbon tax offers the most cost-effective lever to reduce carbon emissions at the scale and speed that is necessary. By correcting a well-known market failure, a carbon tax will send a powerful price signal that harnesses the invisible hand of the marketplace to steer economic actors towards a low-carbon future.

II. A carbon tax should increase every year until emission reduction goals are met and be revenue neutral to avoid debates over the size of government. A consistently rising carbon price will encourage technological innovation and large-scale infrastructure development. It will also accelerate the diffusion of carbon-efficient goods and services.

III. A sufficiently robust and gradually rising carbon tax will replace the need for various carbon regulations that are less efficient. Substituting a price signal for cumbersome regulations will promote economic growth and provide the regulatory certainty companies need for long-term investment in clean-energy alternatives.

IV. To prevent carbon leakage and to protect U.S. competitiveness, a border carbon adjustment system should be established. This system would enhance the competitiveness of American firms that are more energy-efficient than their global competitors. It would also create an incentive for other nations to adopt similar carbon pricing.

V. To maximize the fairness and political viability of a rising carbon tax, all the revenue should be returned directly to U.S. citizens through equal lump-sum rebates. The majority of American families, including the most vulnerable, will benefit financially by receiving more in carbon dividends than they pay in increased energy prices."

Energy Innovation and Carbon Dividend Act
(H.R. 763)

This bill was introduced into the House of Representatives in January 2019. By November 2019, it had over 70 co-sponsors. It will reduce U.S. greenhouse gas emissions 40% below the 2015 level by 2030 and 90% below the 2015 level by 2050. Its key features are:

- The carbon fee starts at $15 per ton and increases by $10 per ton annually. All fees collected are deposited in a Carbon Dividend Trust Fund.

- All net revenue is returned to American households with a full share for each adult and a half share for each child under 19 years old.

- If annual emission reduction targets are not met, the carbon fee increases by $15 per year rather than $10 per year.

- After the 90% emission reduction target is achieved, the carbon fee stops increasing.

No other greenhouse gas regulations are allowed for 10 years. After 10 years, other greenhouse gas regulations are implemented if necessary to meet the annual emission targets.

Carbon-intensive products receive border adjustments to protect the competitiveness of American industry and prevent carbon leakage.

Joel Pett Editorial Cartoon used with the permission of Joel Pett and the Cartoonist Group. All rights reserved.

5.7 BALANCED BUDGET FEEDBACK MECHANISM

The federal debt is growing rapidly because short-term political considerations often outweigh long-term fiscal responsibility.

To address this problem, the BBB tax includes an automatic feedback mechanism to encourage Congress and the president to control spending and balance the federal budget. It works like this:

- If the federal deficit is greater than 3% of GDP and greater than the rate of inflation for two years in a row, then . . .

- The next year, all BBB income tax rates automatically increase by 3% unless (1) the economy was in a recession for at least one quarter (three months) during those two years; or (2) the president and a majority of the House of Representatives, the Senate, and the Federal Reserve Board of Governors all certify that the deficit was necessary due to war or other emergency.

The objective of this feedback mechanism is not to increase tax rates. Rather, its purpose is to provide a powerful incentive for Congress and the president to control spending, balance the federal budget, and prevent a runaway national debt.

Other tax reform proposals generally do not include a provision to control spending. This is a serious flaw. The feedback mechanism proposed here automatically increases taxes if Congress and the president spend too much. The threat of an automatic tax increase will incentivize Congress and the president to reduce waste and control spending.

> "The problem is not that people are taxed too little. The problem is that government spends too much."
>
> — Ronald Reagan

Feedback Mechanism Example

The following example illustrates how the balanced budget feedback mechanism would work: if the federal deficit is 5% of GDP for two consecutive years and if inflation is less than the deficit (say, 2.5% annually), then all BBB income tax rates will automatically increase by 3% unless:

- The economy was in a recession for at least one quarter (three months) during those two years; or

- The president and a majority of the House of Representatives, the Senate, and the Federal Reserve Board of Governors all certify that the deficit was necessary due to war or other emergency.

If the BBB income tax rates increase by 3%, then:

- The tax rate for the lowest income tax bracket will increase from 10% to 10.3%.

- The tax rate for the second lowest tax bracket will increase from 20% to 20.6%.

- The tax rate for the third tax bracket will increase from 28% to 28.8%.

- The tax rate for the highest income tax bracket will increase from 36% to 37.1%.

These new tax rates will remain in effect unless Congress and the president change them or future deficits necessitate another automatic 3% increase in the tax rates.

> Because of economic growth and inflation, Congress and the president can reduce the national debt (as a percentage of GDP) simply by balancing the federal budget. Consider the following example:
>
> If the federal budget is balanced and real economic growth and inflation are each 2% annually, GDP will grow by 4% annually and the national debt will shrink from the current 78% of GDP to:
>
> - 53% of GDP in 10 years
>
> - 36% of GDP in 20 years
>
> This will provide a margin to weather future economic, political, and national security crises.

5.8 PUBLIC DISCLOSURE RULES

The public often feels that politicians rig the tax system to favor themselves and their key supporters. This is damaging to both our democracy and the tax system.

The BBB tax addresses this problem by requiring candidates for high public office to publicly release their tax returns for the five years prior to declaring their candidacy. This includes candidates for (1) president, (2) vice president, (3) the Senate, (4) House of Representatives, (5) governors, and (6) state Senates and Houses of Representatives. If any candidate for high public office does not release their tax forms, the IRS shall release them. The primary objectives of this public disclosure are:

- It will provide the public with important information they need to assess the character of candidates for high public office and possible conflicts of interest.

- It will encourage politicians and others who may want to run for public office to be honest when they prepare their tax returns. It may also discourage unethical (and unserious) candidates from running for high office.

This public disclosure will help ensure that people who hold high public office are honest citizens of good character. This will not prevent corruption—but it is an essential component of the foundation for good governance.

Government must walk a fine line between transparency and protection of private information. Individuals have a right to privacy unless the public good overwhelmingly requires release of private information.

The federal government discloses information on contracts it enters with private parties so the public can confirm that the contracts are not illegal, unethical, or unfair. Americans accept this disclosure in the interest of good governance.

The same principle applies to tax returns. Public disclosure of these tax returns will promote good governance and help prevent illegal, unethical, and unfair collaboration between government officials and special interests and wealthy taxpayers.

5.9 IMPACT OF BBB TAX ON TAXPAYERS

Transitioning from the current tax code to the BBB tax will require several years. During this time, taxpayers will notice the following changes:

Income tax: Most taxpayers will pay less income tax. However, some high-income taxpayers will pay more income tax. The BBB income tax is much simpler than the current income tax, but all taxpayers will need to file a return (even if they owe no taxes) to claim their refundable tax credit and carbon dividends.

Payroll tax: Low-income taxpayers will pay slightly less payroll taxes, because the payroll tax rate is decreased. High-income taxpayers will pay higher payroll taxes, since the cap on taxable income is eliminated.

VAT: The price of goods and services will increase a little as the VAT is implemented. This is because businesses will pass through to consumers the cost of the VAT and carbon fees. However, this cost increase will be small since businesses no longer have to pay corporate income taxes or fund their employees' health care.

Health care: All Americans will receive health care through Medicare Choice; they can either have Medicare or opt out and receive premium support instead. If they choose Medicare, most health care services will require a co-pay, but for most households, the cost of the co-pays will be significantly less than what they currently spend for health care. Also, taxpayers who cannot afford the co-pays can defer them and deduct them from their carbon dividends and refundable tax credits.

Social Security: Since the BBB tax fully funds Social Security, current and future retirees will not have to worry about its financial solvency.

Balanced budgets: Because the BBB tax balances the budget, the federal debt (as a percentage of GDP) will slowly decrease. All Americans should benefit from a lower debt, especially future generations. Congress and the president will pay more attention to balancing the budget since failure to do so will trigger a (small) automatic tax increase.

Carbon dividends: The cost of fossil fuels and energy-intensive products and services will slowly increase due to carbon fees. As the price of fossil fuels increases, more clean and renewable energy alternatives will appear in the marketplace. All revenue from carbon fees will be returned to taxpayers as carbon dividends.

Opportunities: If the BBB tax works as envisioned, it will stimulate economic growth and create more jobs and better opportunities, especially for low-income and middle-income taxpayers.

Twelve Representative Taxpayers:
How the BBB Tax Will Change Their Lives

Now let's examine the impact of the BBB tax on 12 representative taxpayers, as shown in Table 5.9-1. These 12 taxpayers represent three filing status categories and four income levels.

Column 1 is taxpayer filing status. The IRS receives 150 million tax returns annually. Of these, 55 million are from married couples filing jointly, 70 million are from single taxpayers, and 20 million are from heads of households. The only other filing status (married couples filing separately) is not shown here because the IRS receives only a few million of these returns annually.

Column 2 is total income. Four representative income levels are shown: low income (white cells), middle income (dark orange cells), and high and very high income (light orange cells).

Column 3 is labor income. As shown here, low- and middle-income taxpayers earn most of their income from labor. Higher-income taxpayers have more income from other sources. Self-employment income is considered labor income for tax purposes.

Column 4 is payroll tax. It is 14% of labor income. Half is paid by the employer and half is paid by the employee and deducted from the employee's paycheck. This is a flat tax that funds Social Security. All taxpayers with labor income pay this tax.

Table 5.9-1. Twelve Representative Taxpayers

1	2	3	4								
Taxpayer Filing Status	Total Income ($)	Labor Income ($)	Payroll Tax ($)	Taxable Income ($)	Income Tax ($)	Carbon Dividend ($)	VAT Spending ($)	VAT Tax ($)	Excise Taxes ($)	Total Tax ($)	Average Tax Rate (%)
Married Filing Jointly with Two Dependents	40,000	40,000	5,600								
	80,000	72,000	10,080								
	200,000	140,000	19,600								
	500,000	250,000	35,000								
Single Taxpayers	20,000	20,000	2,800								
	40,000	36,000	5,040								
	100,000	70,000	9,800								
	250,000	125,000	17,500								
Head of Household with One Dependent	28,000	28,000	3,920								
	56,000	50,400	7,056								
	140,000	98,000	13,720								
	350,000	175,000	24,500								

Source: The numbers in this table were developed by the author.

Income Tax and Carbon Dividends

Table 5.9-2 is a continuation of Table 5.9-1.

Column 5 is taxable income. It is calculated by subtracting one-half of the payroll tax (the portion paid by the employee) and employee contributions to retirement plans from total income. For this example, taxable income is calculated using the following employee retirement contributions: (1) zero for low-income taxpayers (white cells), (2) 4% of labor income for middle-income taxpayers (dark orange cells), and (3) 8% of labor income for high-income and very-high-income taxpayers (light orange cells).

Column 6 is income tax. It is calculated based on the tax rates in Table 5.1-1 and the refundable $1,000 tax credit. As this column shows, low-income taxpayers pay no income tax and receive a refundable tax credit. Middle-income taxpayers pay only a little income tax. High-income and very-high-income taxpayers pay much higher income tax.

Column 7 is the carbon dividend. Its size will vary from year to year, but for this example, a value of $1,000 per person is used. The carbon dividend is calculated by multiplying the number of taxpayers and dependents by $1,000. The numbers shown in this column are annual values, even though carbon dividends may be paid quarterly or monthly.

Table 5.9-2. Income Tax and Carbon Dividend for 12 Taxpayers

1	2	3	4	5	6	7					
Taxpayer Filing Status	Total Income ($)	Labor Income ($)	Payroll Tax ($)	Taxable Income ($)	Income Tax ($)	Carbon Dividend ($)	VAT Spending ($)	VAT Tax ($)	Excise Taxes ($)	Total Tax ($)	Average Tax Rate (%)
Married Filing Jointly with Two Dependents	40,000	40,000	5,600	37,200	-3,280	4,000					
	80,000	72,000	10,080	72,080	208	4,000					
	200,000	140,000	19,600	179,000	20,800	4,000					
	500,000	250,000	35,000	462,500	113,100	4,000					
Single Taxpayers	20,000	20,000	2,800	18,600	-640	1,000					
	40,000	36,000	5,040	36,040	1,104	1,000					
	100,000	70,000	9,800	89,500	11,400	1,000					
	250,000	125,000	17,500	231,250	57,550	1,000					
Head of Household with One Dependent	28,000	28,000	3,920	26,040	-1,496	2,000					
	56,000	50,400	7,056	50,456	945.6	2,000					
	140,000	98,000	13,720	125,300	15,360	2,000					
	350,000	175,000	24,500	323,750	79,970	2,000					

Source: The numbers in this table were developed by the author.

VAT and Excise Taxes

Table 5.9-3 is a continuation of Table 5.9-2.

Column 8 is VAT spending. This is an estimate of how much each taxpayer spends on products and services subject to the VAT. It is calculated by adding taxable income and the carbon dividend and subtracting income tax and savings outside of retirement accounts. For this example, VAT spending is calculated using the following savings rates: (1) zero for low-income and middle-income taxpayers, (2) 5% of taxable income for high-income taxpayers, and (3) 10% of taxable income for very-high-income taxpayers.

Column 9 is the VAT tax. It is 13% of VAT spending. This tax is paid by businesses and passed through to consumers in the cost of goods and services. It is a flat tax that funds Medicare Choice.

Column 10 is excise taxes, including carbon fees. Excise taxes and carbon fees are paid by businesses and passed through to consumers in the cost of goods and services. The amount of excise taxes paid by taxpayers will depend on the products and services they purchase. For this example, excise taxes are estimated as follows: (1) 4% of VAT spending for low-income taxpayers, (2) 3% of VAT spending for middle-income taxpayers, and (3) 2% of VAT spending for high-income and very-high-income taxpayers. Most of these excise taxes are carbon fees, which are returned to taxpayers via quarterly or monthly carbon dividend checks.

Table 5.9-3. VAT and Excise Taxes for 12 Taxpayers

1	2	3	4	5	6	7	8	9	10		
Taxpayer Filing Status	Total Income ($)	Labor Income ($)	Payroll Tax ($)	Taxable Income ($)	Income Tax ($)	Carbon Dividend ($)	VAT Spending ($)	VAT Tax ($)	Excise Taxes ($)	Total Tax ($)	Average Tax Rate (%)
Married Filing Jointly with Two Dependents	40,000	40,000	5,600	37,200	-3,280	4,000	44,480	5,782	1,779		
	80,000	72,000	10,080	72,080	208	4,000	75,872	9,863	2,276		
	200,000	140,000	19,600	179,000	20,800	4,000	153,250	19,923	3,065		
	500,000	250,000	35,000	462,500	113,100	4,000	307,150	39,930	6,143		
Single Taxpayers	20,000	20,000	2,800	18,600	-640	1,000	20,240	2,631	810		
	40,000	36,000	5,040	36,040	1,104	1,000	35,936	4,672	1,078		
	100,000	70,000	9,800	89,500	11,400	1,000	74,625	9,701	1,493		
	250,000	125,000	17,500	231,250	57,550	1,000	151,575	19,705	3,032		
Head of Household with One Dependent	28,000	28,000	3,920	26,040	-1,496	2,000	29,536	3,840	1,181		
	56,000	50,400	7,056	50,456	945.6	2,000	51,510	6,696	1,545		
	140,000	98,000	13,720	125,300	15,360	2,000	105,675	13,738	2,114		
	350,000	175,000	24,500	323,750	79,970	2,000	213,405	27,743	4,268		

Source: The numbers in this table were developed by the author.

Total Tax and Average Tax Rates

Table 5.9-4 is a continuation of Table 5.9-3.

Column 11 shows total tax. It is calculated by adding the payroll tax, income tax, VAT, and excise tax, and subtracting the carbon dividend. Column 12 shows average tax rate. It is calculated by dividing total tax by total income. Key items to note are:

- Low-income taxpayers pay some tax, but less than the cost of their Social Security and Medicare Choice benefits. Their average tax rates are 15% to 23% in this example.

- Middle-income taxpayers pay higher taxes, enough to fund a substantial part of their Social Security and Medicare Choice benefits. Their average tax rates are 23% to 27% in this example.

- High-income and very-high-income taxpayers pay the highest taxes. They pay more than the cost of their Social Security and Medicare Choice benefits. Their average tax rates are 30% to 39%.

Although not shown on Table 5.9-4, taxpayers with extremely high incomes will pay higher tax rates, generally in the range of 40% to 45%.

The BBB tax is unapologetically progressive and egalitarian. It is progressive because the average tax rate increases with income; it is egalitarian because almost everyone pays taxes.

Table 5.9-4. Total Tax and Average Tax Rate for 12 Taxpayers

1	2	3	4	5	6	7	8	9	10	11	12
Taxpayer Filing Status	Total Income ($)	Labor Income ($)	Payroll Tax ($)	Taxable Income ($)	Income Tax ($)	Carbon Dividend ($)	VAT Spending ($)	VAT Tax ($)	Excise Taxes ($)	Total Tax ($)	Average Tax Rate (%)
Married Filing Jointly with Two Dependents	40,000	40,000	5,600	37,200	-3,280	4,000	44,480	5,782	1,779	5,882	15%
	80,000	72,000	10,080	72,080	208	4,000	75,872	9,863	2,276	18,428	23%
	200,000	140,000	19,600	179,000	20,800	4,000	153,250	19,923	3,065	59,388	30%
	500,000	250,000	35,000	462,500	113,100	4,000	307,150	39,930	6,143	190,173	38%
Single Taxpayers	20,000	20,000	2,800	18,600	-640	1,000	20,240	2,631	810	4,601	23%
	40,000	36,000	5,040	36,040	1,104	1,000	35,936	4,672	1,078	10,894	27%
	100,000	70,000	9,800	89,500	11,400	1,000	74,625	9,701	1,493	31,394	31%
	250,000	125,000	17,500	231,250	57,550	1,000	151,575	19,705	3,032	96,786	39%
Head of Household with One Dependent	28,000	28,000	3,920	26,040	-1,496	2,000	29,536	3,840	1,181	5,445	19%
	56,000	50,400	7,056	50,456	945.6	2,000	51,510	6,696	1,545	14,243	25%
	140,000	98,000	13,720	125,300	15,360	2,000	105,675	13,738	2,114	42,931	31%
	350,000	175,000	24,500	323,750	79,970	2,000	213,405	27,743	4,268	134,481	38%

Source: The numbers in this table were developed by the author.

"Out-of-Pocket" Taxes

The total tax and average tax rates on the previous page (Table 5.9-4, columns 11 and 12) include two kinds of taxes: (1) "out-of-pocket" tax paid directly by taxpayers, and (2) taxes embedded in the cost of products and services.

Column 13 in Table 5.9-5 shows out-of-pocket tax. It is calculated by adding one-half of the payroll tax (the employee contribution) and income tax and subtracting the carbon dividend. It is much less than the total tax in Table 5.9-4. Column 14 shows the average out-of-pocket tax rate. It is calculated by dividing out-of-pocket tax by total income.

Embedded taxes are those that are included in the cost of products and services. The BBB tax has more embedded taxes than the current tax code for the following reasons:

- The BBB tax includes two major new business taxes: the VAT and carbon fees. These new business taxes will add (on average) roughly 15% to business costs.

- The BBB tax eliminates two major business expenses: the corporate income tax and employee health care. This will reduce business costs (on average) by about 8%.

As a result, businesses will probably increase the cost of their products and services roughly 7% (15% – 8%). If the BBB tax is implemented over seven years, the cost of products and services will likely increase by about 1% annually during the seven-year transition. However, this will be offset by lower out-of-pocket health care costs.

Table 5.9-5. "Out of Pocket" Tax for 12 Taxpayers

1	2	3	4	5	6	7	8	9	10	13	14
Taxpayer Filing Status	Total Income ($)	Labor Income ($)	Payroll Tax ($)	Taxable Income ($)	Income Tax ($)	Carbon Dividend ($)	VAT Spending ($)	VAT Tax ($)	Excise Taxes ($)	Out-of-Pocket Tax ($)	Average Tax Rate (%)
Married Filing Jointly with Two Dependents	40,000	40,000	5,600	37,200	-3,280	4,000	44,480	5,782	1,334	-4,480	-11%
	80,000	72,000	10,080	72,080	208	4,000	75,872	9,863	2,276	1,248	2%
	200,000	140,000	19,600	179,000	20,800	4,000	153,250	19,923	4,598	26,600	13%
	500,000	250,000	35,000	462,500	113,100	4,000	307,150	39,930	9,215	126,600	25%
Single Taxpayers	20,000	20,000	2,800	18,600	-640	1,000	20,240	2,631	607	-240	-1%
	40,000	36,000	5,040	36,040	1,104	1,000	35,936	4,672	1,078	2,624	7%
	100,000	70,000	9,800	89,500	11,400	1,000	74,625	9,701	2,239	15,300	15%
	250,000	125,000	17,500	231,250	57,550	1,000	151,575	19,705	4,547	65,300	26%
Head of Household with One Dependent	28,000	28,000	3,920	26,040	-1,496	2,000	29,536	3,840	886	-1,536	-5%
	56,000	50,400	7,056	50,456	945.6	2,000	51,510	6,696	1,545	2,474	4%
	140,000	98,000	13,720	125,300	15,360	2,000	105,675	13,738	3,170	20,220	14%
	350,000	175,000	24,500	323,750	79,970	2,000	213,405	27,743	6,402	90,220	26%

Source: The numbers in this table were developed by the author.

5.10 IMPLEMENTATION SCHEDULE

Several years will be required to implement the BBB tax. The following is an example schedule:

Year 1:

- Implement the new individual income tax.

- Implement changes to the estate and excise taxes (except carbon dividends).

Year 2:

- Eliminate the corporate income tax.

- Initiate the VAT with a 4% tax rate (earmarked for health care).

- Change the payroll tax to 14% (earmarked for Social Security).

- Implement carbon dividends.

Year 3: Increase the VAT to 7% and extend Medicare to include ages 50–65.

Year 5: Increase the VAT to 10% and extend Medicare to include ages 0–25.

Year 7: Increase the VAT to 13% and extend Medicare to include all ages.

States should reform their tax systems in parallel with implementing the BBB tax. Ideally, states will simplify and improve their tax systems using the federal tax system as a model. For example, states could:

- Simplify their individual income taxes by taxing all types of income at the same (progressive) rates and eliminating all itemized deductions and most tax credits, tax preferences, and loopholes.

- Replace their sales tax and corporate income tax with a broad-based VAT similar to the federal VAT. Most states have (narrow) sales taxes with tax rates of 5% to 10% and collect little revenue from corporate income taxes. Therefore, a (broad) VAT with a lower tax rate can replace both their sales tax and corporate income tax.

6 EVALUATION AND IMPROVEMENT

SE uses an iterative process to improve product design. Each design iteration is evaluated against the objectives and design alternatives. This process provides insights regarding a design's strengths and weaknesses, and often leads to better designs.

The same process can be applied to the tax code. The following pages illustrate this process for the BBB tax. Four types of evaluations are presented. First, the BBB tax is evaluated against the eight tax reform objectives. Second, it is compared to the current tax code. Third, potential problem areas are identified and discussed. Fourth, the BBB tax is compared with seven alternative tax reform proposals.

SE Process for Tax Reform

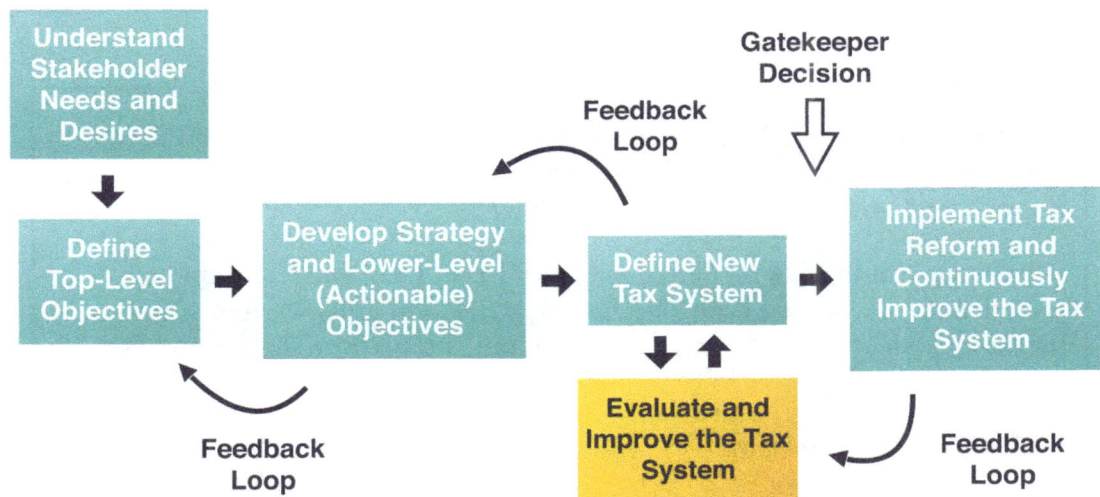

Objective #1: Fiscally Responsible

Objective: Tax reform should balance the federal budget and reduce the national debt.

Advantages:

- The BBB tax balances the federal budget.

- The balanced budget feedback mechanism encourages Congress and the president to control spending and maintain a balanced budget.

Disadvantages:

- The cost of Medicare Choice is uncertain.

Summary: 4 (on a 5-point scale, with 5 being best)

Key: Very good = 5, Good = 4, Fair = 3, Poor = 2, Very poor = 1, Unacceptable = 0

The objective of the BBB tax is to balance the federal budget and shrink the national debt as a percent of GDP. However, the national debt will shrink even if the federal government runs a small deficit.

For example, if the federal deficit averages 1% of GDP and real economic growth and inflation are each 2% annually, GDP will grow 4% annually and the national debt (as a percentage of GDP) will shrink from the current 78% of GDP to:

- 61% of GDP in 10 years

- 49% of GDP in 20 years

The balanced budget feedback mechanism (Chapter 5.7) is designed to ensure that the federal debt (as a percentage of GDP) will not increase significantly except in a severe recession or national emergency.

Objective #2: Pro-Growth

Objective: Tax reform should support economic growth, productivity, and competitiveness.

Advantages:

- The BBB tax stimulates sustainable growth by eliminating the corporate income tax, balancing the federal budget, and controlling the cost of health care.

- Since the VAT is a tax on consumption, it will encourage savings and investment. This will be good for long-term growth.

Disadvantages:

- The VAT will decrease consumer spending. This will reduce short-term growth.

Summary: 4 (on a 5-point scale, with 5 being best)

Robust economic growth is key to successful tax reform. The Congressional Budget Office (CBO) projects that the U.S. economy will grow slightly less than 2% annually for the next 30 years. I think we should try to achieve at least 2.5% to 3% annual growth for the next 30 years. The following example illustrates the importance of growth:

- If real economic growth is 2% annually, real GDP will grow by 22% in 10 years and 81% in 30 years.

- If real economic growth is 2.5% annually, real GDP will grow by 28% in 10 years and 110% in 30 years.

- If real economic growth is 3% annually, real GDP will grow by 34% in 10 years and 143% in 30 years.

This difference is significant. If the economy grows 2.5% to 3% annually rather than 2% annually, this will create more jobs, with higher pay, and the national debt (as a percentage of GDP) will shrink faster.

Objective #3: Realistic

Objective: Tax reform should be evaluated with realistic assumptions.

Advantages:

- The BBB tax uses realistic assumptions.

Disadvantages:

- The cost of Medicare Choice is uncertain.

Summary: 4 (on a 5-point scale, with 5 being best)

The VAT and Medicare Choice are radical departures from the current U.S. tax and health care systems, so how can we be sure they are based on realistic assumptions?

Even though the VAT and Medicare Choice are new for the United States, they are similar to tax and health care systems used in other countries. The assumptions used here are realistic since they are based on actual experience in many countries.

Objective #4: Comprehensive

Objective: Reform should be comprehensive—tax cuts are not tax reform.

Advantages:

The BBB tax is comprehensive reform. It fixes all major problems with the current tax code. It is comprehensive for the following reasons:

- It balances the federal budget and includes a feedback mechanism to encourage Congress and the president to control spending.

- It improves the U.S. health care system (by funding Medicare Choice) and restores Social Security to financial health without increasing the burden on taxpayers.

- It stimulates economic growth by decreasing tax rates and replacing the corporate income tax with a more efficient VAT.

- It simplifies the tax code by eliminating all itemized deductions and most tax credits, tax preferences, and loopholes.

- It increases funding for infrastructure (the Transportation Trust Fund) and for education (the Education Trust Fund).

- It includes carbon dividends, an economically efficient, bipartisan solution for climate change.

Disadvantages:

- The BBB tax may be too great a change and could result in unintended consequences.

Summary: 5 (on a 5-point scale, with 5 being best)

Objective #5: Fair

Objective: The benefits of tax reform should be widely shared, with the most economically vulnerable protected.

Advantages:

Fairness is subjective, so each person must decide for themselves whether a tax is fair. The BBB tax aims to achieve fairness as follows:

- It treats all taxpayers in the same way, except for the public disclosure rules that apply only to candidates for high-level office.

- It taxes everyone in accordance with their ability to pay. The BBB income tax is progressive, while the VAT and payroll taxes are flat.

- It provides a strong social safety net. This is especially important for low-income and middle-income taxpayers, but even high-income taxpayers may need help at some time in their lives.

- It creates better opportunities by encouraging economic growth and balanced budgets.

Disadvantages:

- Some people will consider the BBB tax unfair since it eliminates the corporate income tax.

- Some people may consider it unfair because it is too progressive or not progressive enough.

- Special interest groups may consider it unfair since it eliminates itemized deductions, tax credits, tax preferences, and loopholes which they think are justified.

Summary: 4 (on a 5-point scale, with 5 being best)

Objective #6: Simple

Objective: Tax reform should simplify the tax code.

Advantages:

- The BBB tax simplifies individual income taxes and eliminates corporate income taxes. Table 6-1 illustrates the simplicity of the BBB income tax calculation.

Disadvantages:

- The VAT and carbon dividends add complexity.

Summary: 4 (on a 5-point scale, with 5 being best)

Table 6-1. Example Income Tax Returns

Line	Name: John and Jane Doe Children: Two Filing Status: Married, filing jointly	Low Income Example	Middle Income Example	High Income Example
1	Number of taxpayers + dependents	4	4	4
2	Taxable income (total from all sources)	$40,000	$80,000	$200,000
3	Tax (from Table 5.1-2)	$1,000	$5,000	$30,600
4	Tax credit ($1,000 x line 1)	$4,000	$4,000	$4,000
5	Net tax (line 3 - line 4)	-$3,000	$1,000	$26,600
6	Income tax withheld	$0	$3,000	$28,000
7	Tax refund (line 6 - line 5)*	$3,000	$2,000	$1,400
8	Tax owed (line 5 - line 6)	0	0	0

*In addition to these income tax refunds, every family of four receives quarterly or monthly carbon dividend checks worth about $2,000 to $6,000 per year ($500 to $1,500 per person), regardless of income.

Objective #7: Permanent

Objective: Reform should enact permanent changes to the tax code.

Advantages:

- The BBB tax is permanent (no feature expires).

Disadvantages:

- The feedback mechanism increases uncertainty regarding future tax rates, but it reduces uncertainty about federal budget deficits.

- Because the BBB tax is a major change, it may result in unintended consequences and require additional changes or adjustments.

Summary: 4 (on a 5-point scale, with 5 being best)

Objective #8: Bipartisan

Objective: Bipartisan tax reform is more durable and long-lasting.

Advantages: The key features of the BBB tax which may receive bipartisan support are as follows:

- It balances the federal budget.

- It simplifies the tax code.

- It restores Social Security to financial health.

- It fixes the health care system with an approach that both parties may be able to accept.

- It addresses climate change with a market-based approach (carbon dividends).

- Both parties have historically opposed a VAT. However, Democrats may support it as a way to fund Medicare Choice, and Republicans may support it as a way to eliminate the corporate income tax.

Disadvantages: The features of the BBB tax that are likely to be most problematic for Democrats and Republicans are as follows:

- Democrats will dislike eliminating the corporate income tax.

- Republicans will dislike that the BBB tax expands the role of federal government (for health care) and increases federal tax revenue (to pay for health care).

- Both parties will probably struggle with the idea of eliminating all itemized deductions and most tax credits, tax preferences, and loopholes.

Summary: 4 (on a 5-point scale, with 5 being best)

It is impossible to predict whether the BBB tax will receive bipartisan support. Nevertheless, I chose a rating of 4 because the BBB tax achieves the most important objectives of conservatives, liberals, and moderates.

Key Differences Between TCJA and BBB Tax

Table 6-2 summarizes the key features of the current tax code versus the BBB tax. The current tax code is the Tax Cuts and Jobs Act (TCJA) enacted in late 2017. Key items to note in this table are:

- The BBB tax is bipartisan and balances the federal budget. The TCJA is not bipartisan and does not balance the budget.

- The TCJA individual income tax has many itemized deductions, tax credits, and tax preferences. The BBB tax has only one tax credit (the $1,000 refundable tax credit).

- The TCJA has a corporate income tax with a tax rate of 21% and many deductions and credits. The BBB tax has a VAT with a tax rate of 13% and no corporate income tax.

- The BBB tax funds Medicare Choice and fixes Social Security. It also includes carbon dividends, a balanced budget feedback mechanism, and public disclosure rules. The TCJA has none of these.

Table 6-2. Key Differences Between TCJA and BBB Tax

Objective	Key Features	
	Current Tax Code (TCJA)	BBB Tax
Bipartisan?	No	Yes
Balanced budget?	No	Yes
Individual income tax - Tax rates - Itemized deductions - Standard deduction - Tax credits - Tax preferences	12% to 37% Many Yes Many Many	10% to 36% None Larger One Few
Corporate income tax - Tax rate - Itemized deductions and credits	21% Many	No corporate income tax
VAT tax rate	No VAT	13%
Funds universal health care?	No	Yes
Payroll tax rate	15.3%	14%
Social Security benefits sustainable?	No	Yes
Carbon dividends?	No	Yes

Comparison of TCJA and BBB Tax

Table 6-3 summarizes my evaluation of the BBB tax versus the TCJA (Tax Cuts and Jobs Act) enacted in 2017. Key items to note in this table are:

- For the purposes of this evaluation, all eight objectives are weighted equally, with a maximum value of five points each. The maximum available points is therefore 40 (8 x 5). The weight given to each objective should be based on its level of importance. This is discussed further on the next page.

- My evaluation indicates that the BBB tax is better than the current tax code. You are encouraged to perform your own evaluation and draw your own conclusions.

- The numbers in this table are subjective and are less important than the insights gained while performing the evaluation. One of my insights is that the BBB tax addresses the eight objectives more evenly than the current tax code.

If the objectives change, the evaluation results will also change. For example, if the only objectives are (1) low taxes, and (2) near-term economic growth, then the TCJA may be better than the BBB tax. This illustrates why the first three steps of the SE process (the definition of requirements) are so important. The quality of a product (an aircraft, spacecraft, or tax system) is largely determined by the quality of the requirements established for it.

Table 6-3. Comparison of TCJA and BBB Tax

Objective	Maximum Points	Evaluation Results	
		BBB Tax	TCJA
Fiscally responsible	5	4	1
Pro-growth	5	4	4
Realistic	5	4	4
Comprehensive	5	5	2
Fair	5	4	1
Simple	5	4	2
Permanent	5	4	2
Bipartisan	5	4	2
Total	40	33	18

Source: The author prepared this table. You are encouraged to perform your own evaluation.
Key: Very good = 5, Good = 4, Fair = 3, Poor = 2, Very poor = 1, Unacceptable = 0

How Does the Evaluation Change
If Objectives Are Weighted Differently?

Table 6-4 is similar to Table 6-3, but now four of the objectives are weighted to be twice as important. As a result, the maximum available points is 60 (four objectives weighted at 10 points each and four objectives weighted at 5 points each).

My evaluation indicates that the BBB tax is better than the current tax code with these weights or any other reasonable weighting factors. You are encouraged to perform your own evaluation and draw your own conclusions.

SE tries to find solutions that are insensitive to slight changes in the weights given to each objective. The best way to do this is to find solutions that satisfy all objectives as much as possible, rather than just one or two objectives.

Table 6-4. Evaluation Results with Different Weighting Factors

Objective	Maximum Points	Evaluation Results	
		BBB Tax	TCJA
Fiscally responsible	10	8	2
Pro-growth	10	8	8
Realistic	5	4	4
Comprehensive	5	5	2
Fair	10	8	2
Simple	5	4	2
Permanent	5	4	2
Bipartisan	10	8	4
Total	60	49	26

Source: The author prepared this table. You are encouraged to do your own evaluation.
Key: Very good = 5 out of 5 or 10 out of 10
    Good = 4 out of 5 or 8 out of 10
    Fair = 3 out of 5 or 6 out of 10
    Poor = 2 out of 5 or 4 out of 10
    Very poor = 1 out of 5 or 2 out of 10
    Unacceptable = 0 out of 5 or 0 out of 10

Some Stakeholders Will Dislike the BBB Tax

Although the BBB tax appears better than the current tax code when evaluated against a broad spectrum of objectives, many stakeholders who are focused on one or two objectives may dislike the BBB tax. Following are several examples:

- **Anti-tax advocates:** Many Americans are opposed to any increase in taxes. The BBB tax increases federal taxes to pay for Medicare Choice and balance the federal budget. Anti-tax advocates may dislike the BBB tax because it increases taxes. **Rebuttal:** The BBB tax does not increase the total burden on taxpayers, as Table 4-3 shows. Instead, it shifts responsibility for funding health care from businesses, states, and individuals to the federal government.

- **Health care industry:** Medicare Choice will force the health care industry to reduce costs. Many companies and people in the health care industry may resist this change. **Rebuttal:** The U.S. health care system must be improved. The health care industry can either lead the change or be dragged into it and incur a public relations nightmare. If done right, Medicare Choice can address many problems that currently plague the health care industry and create opportunities for innovative health care providers.

- **Health care skeptics:** Some people will resist Medicare Choice because they are skeptical that it can control costs or improve health care. **Rebuttal:** Other countries have shown that single-payer health care systems can reduce costs and improve health care outcomes. The balanced budget feedback mechanism is an important part of the BBB tax because it gives politicians a powerful incentive to control spending.

- **Conservatives:** Most conservatives do not like big government. They may object to Medicare Choice and the VAT as an unreasonable expansion of government. **Rebuttal:** Even though the BBB tax expands the role of the federal government, it limits this expansion by (1) eliminating the corporate income tax, (2) earmarking VAT revenue for Medicare Choice (so it cannot be used to expand the government in other areas), and (3) providing a balanced budget feedback mechanism to encourage Congress and the president to control spending.

- **Liberals:** Many liberals think the top tax rate for high-income taxpayers and the corporate income tax should be increased. They may object to the BBB tax because it reduces the top individual income tax rate and eliminates the corporate income tax. **Rebuttal:** The BBB tax is more progressive than the current tax system. High-income taxpayers will pay more income taxes (even with the lower top tax rate) since the BBB tax eliminates itemized deductions and most tax credits, preferences, and loopholes. The VAT is also progressive because it funds Medicare Choice. It is more progressive than the current corporate income tax and health care system, which impose immense financial burdens on low-income and middle-income taxpayers.

Some Stakeholders Will Dislike the BBB Tax (continued)

- **Climate change skeptics:** Those who do not believe in climate change may object to the BBB tax because it includes carbon dividends. **Rebuttal:** Even people who do not believe in climate change should support carbon dividends for three reasons. First, carbon dividends are preferable to heavy-handed regulations to address climate change. Second, carbon dividends provide a convenient way to ensure that taxpayers file income tax returns and pay their Medicare Choice co-pays. Third, carbon dividends will reduce air pollution and encourage an economically efficient transition from fossil fuels to renewable energy.

- **Special interests:** Special interest groups and non-profit organizations may object to the BBB tax since it eliminates itemized deductions, tax credits, preferences, and loopholes they consider important to their well-being. **Rebuttal:** Other countries have eliminated or reduced itemized deductions, tax credits, preferences, and loopholes, and their citizens have continued to invest in businesses, purchase homes, and donate to charities. Fear of the unknown is the greatest obstacle to change.

- **Other countries:** Many countries may object to the BBB tax because it eliminates the corporate income tax. That will make the U.S. a magnet for business investment and place them at a competitive disadvantage. **Rebuttal:** Other countries have been reducing their corporate income taxes for many years, and if this trend continues, they too will soon eliminate corporate income taxes. The corporate income tax is a dinosaur in the modern world with so many large multi-national corporations.

The foregoing discussion highlights some of the reasons why people may dislike the BBB tax. These concerns are all valid if considered in isolation. Surprisingly, almost none of the many people who reviewed this book prior to publication expressed any of these concerns. This suggests to me that they took a broad view of the BBB tax and considered it as whole, rather than focusing on objections that might be raised regarding specific provisions. My hope is that others will do the same because, as Tables 6-2 through 6-4 show, the BBB tax has many advantages, if viewed in its entirety.

Can the BBB Tax Be Improved?

Yes! The BBB tax is only a "first attempt" to develop a better tax code using SE. It can undoubtedly be improved. The next chapter describes how Congress and the president can use SE to improve the BBB tax and implement bipartisan tax reform.

The BBB tax is proposed as the starting point for comprehensive tax reform. Many alternatives should be considered to improve it. Here are four examples:

Individual income tax: The tax rates, tax brackets, and the size of the standard deduction and refundable tax credit can be changed to make the BBB tax more or less progressive. For example, if the top two tax rates (28% and 36%) are increased to 30% and 40%, the standard deduction and refundable tax credit can be increased, making the BBB tax more progressive.

Corporate income tax: Instead of eliminating the corporate income tax, its tax rate can be reduced. For example, if the corporate income tax is reduced to 10% instead of being eliminated, the total tax on corporate profits will be 23% (10% from the corporate income tax and 13% from the VAT).

Payroll taxes: The payroll tax can be reduced or eliminated by increasing the VAT. This will reduce the tax on labor income and increase the tax on other VAT items such as corporate profit, fringe benefits, and interest income. For example, the payroll tax can be eliminated by increasing the VAT tax rate from 13% to 22%. The tax rate on corporate profits will then be 22%. In this case, VAT revenue will be sufficient to fund both Social Security and Medicare Choice.

Medicare Choice cost target: The Medicare Choice cost target of 14% of GDP can be increased or decreased to allocate more or less of GDP to health care. Of course, if it is increased, then additional revenue must be obtained to balance the budget. This additional revenue might be obtained by (1) increasing the VAT tax rate, or (2) earmarking revenue from a (small) corporate income tax for Medicare Choice.

These are just four examples of many alternatives that could be considered to optimize the BBB tax.

Is the Proposed Tax Reform Too Radical?

No! When I first developed the BBB tax, I thought it might be too radical to be implemented in a single tax reform bill. But as I studied the history of taxation, I realized that the most successful tax reforms have all been radical.

Experience shows that radical tax reform is often easier than incremental tax reform. The following quotes illustrate this:

- New Zealand parliamentarian Maurice McTigue explained how they were able to replace their decrepit tax code with a new tax system: "A key reason was that we did it big. We changed almost everything at once. And that's an important lesson: if you're going to do tax reform, you'd better make it a large tax reform. That way, for every change a taxpayer doesn't like, there's something else in the package that he wants."

- Senator Bill Bradley made the following statement after the U.S. implemented the Tax Reform Act of 1986: "You can't just tinker. Facing a huge, almost incomprehensible system, you have to take it on. Your goal has to be to fix the whole damn thing."

No one who reviewed this book prior to publication commented that the BBB tax is too radical. This surprised me, but it is consistent with the lessons learned from the history of taxation. So, after studying past tax reforms and receiving feedback from reviewers, I think the BBB tax is not too radical. In fact, its greatest strength may be that it *is* radical.

Tax Reform Alternatives

While I was writing this book, tax policy experts from seven public policy organizations independently developed tax reform proposals under the sponsorship of the Peter G. Peterson Foundation *Solutions Initiative 2019*. The goal of this program is to "inform the national conversation in advance of the 2020 election" and identify a "better course for America with less debt, stronger economic growth, broader prosperity, and enhanced economic opportunity."

The seven organizations that developed tax reform proposals are: the Center for American Progress, the Bipartisan Policy Center, the Manhattan Institute, the American Enterprise Institute, the Economic Policy Institute, the Progressive Policy Institute, and the American Action Forum. These organizations span the political spectrum: two are liberal, two are conservative, and three are centrist.

The Peter G. Peterson Foundation enlisted the Tax Policy Center to evaluate and compare the seven tax reform proposals. The results are summarized in Figure 6-1 and in the next three pages. One of the most significant features of these tax reform proposals is that they all reduce the national debt compared to current policy, as shown in Figure 6-1.

Figure 6-1. All Seven Tax Reform Proposals Reduce the Debt

Debt Held by the Public (% of GDP)

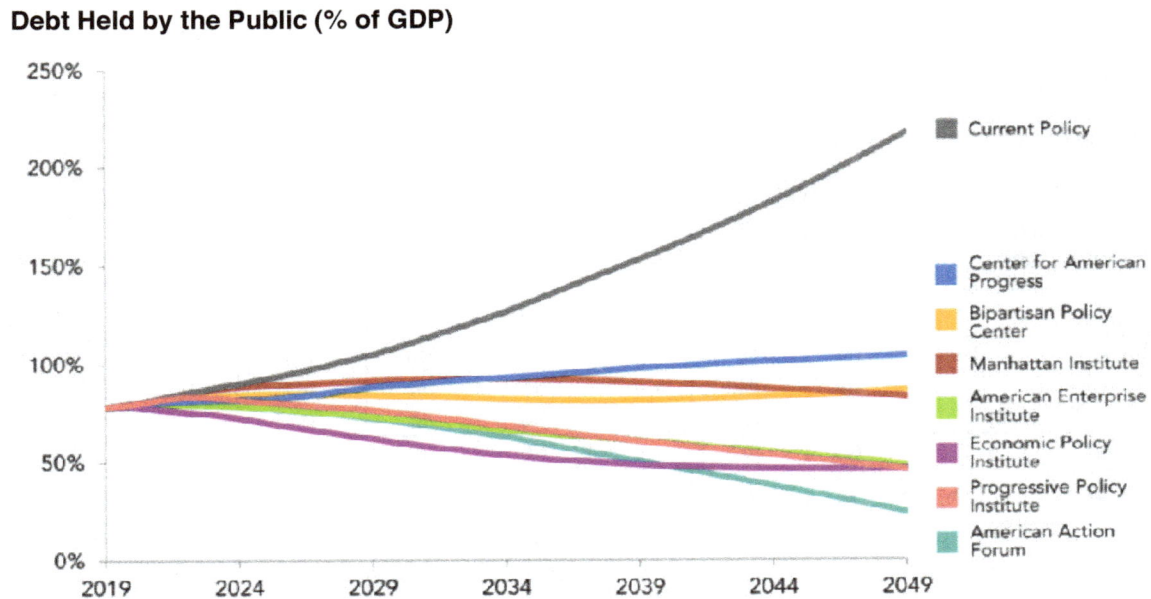

Source: Peter G. Peterson Foundation, *Solutions Initiative 2019: Charting a Sustainable Future,* June 2019. Used with permission of the Peter G. Peterson Foundation.

Comparison of Tax Reform Alternatives

Table 6-5 summarizes the key features of the BBB tax and the seven alternative tax reform proposals. The key items to note on this table are discussed below and on the following two pages.

National debt: All seven tax reform alternatives significantly reduce the debt versus the current tax code. Four balance (or nearly balance) the budget and reduce the debt to less than 50% of GDP. The other three reduce the deficit compared to current policy, but do not balance the budget. The BBB tax balances the budget.

Table 6-5. Comparison of Tax Reform Alternatives

Features	BBB Tax	Seven Tax Reform Alternatives						
		American Action Forum	American Enterprise Institute	Manhattan Institute	Bipartisan Policy Center	Progressive Policy Institute	Center for American Progress	Economic Policy Institute
Balanced Budget?	Yes	Yes	Nearly	No	No	Nearly	No	Nearly
Debt in 2049 (% of GDP)	25%	24%	48%	83%	86%	46%	104%	46%
Universal Health Care?	Yes	No	No	No	No	No	Yes	Yes
Employers Provide Insurance for Employees?	Option	Yes	Yes	Yes	Yes	Yes	No	No
Replace Medicare with Premium Support System?	Option	Yes	Yes	Yes	No	No	No	No
Individual Income Tax Top Tax Rate	36%	40%	35%	37%	37%	50%	45%	45%
Deductions, Tax Credits and Tax Preferences	Very Few	Few	Few	Many	Many	Many	Few	Few
Corporate Income Tax Rate	0%	20%	21%	21%	25%	28%	30%	35%
VAT Tax Rate	13%	0%	0%	0%	0%	?	0%	0%
Restore Social Security Financial Solvency?	Yes	Yes	Yes	Yes	Yes	Yes	Yes	Yes
Payroll Tax Rate	14%	15%	15%	17%	16%	VAT	16%	18%
Increase Discretionary Spending?	Yes	Yes	No	Yes	Yes	Yes	Yes	Yes
Address Climate Change?	Yes	Yes	Yes	No	Yes	Yes	Yes	Yes
Carbon Tax?	No	Yes	Yes	No	Yes	Yes	Yes	Yes
Carbon Dividends?	Yes	No	No	No	No	No	No	No
Bipartisan?	Yes	No	No	No	Yes	No	No	No

Source: This table was developed by the author based on an analysis performed by the Tax Policy Center and posted on the Peter G. Peterson Foundation website in a report titled *Solutions Initiative 2019: Charting a Sustainable Future*. All percentages have been rounded to the nearest whole number.

Comparison of Tax Reform Alternatives (continued)

Health care: Two of the alternatives include universal health care (Medicare-for-All). The other five continue to rely on employers to provide health care insurance for most Americans. Two of these five proposals make relatively small changes to Medicare, Medicaid, and Obamacare. The other three replace Medicare with a "premium support" system and make small changes to Medicaid and Obamacare.

The BBB tax includes universal health care (Medicare Choice).

Individual income tax: Four of the alternatives keep the top tax rate similar to the current maximum tax rate (37%). The other three increase the top tax rate to between 45% and 50%.

Four of the alternatives significantly reduce itemized deductions, tax credits, and tax preferences. The other three retain most deductions, credits, and preferences.

The BBB tax reduces the top tax rate slightly and eliminates all itemized deductions and most tax credits, tax preferences, and loopholes.

Corporate income tax: Three of the alternatives keep the corporate income tax rate similar to the current tax rate (21%). The other four increase the corporate income tax rate to between 25% and 35%.

The BBB tax eliminates the corporate income tax and replaces it with a VAT with a tax rate of 13%.

Social Security: All seven alternatives restore Social Security to financial health. Most achieve this by a combination of small benefit cuts and small increases in payroll taxes. One plan replaces the payroll tax with a VAT. Although not shown in this table, four of the alternative tax reform plans eliminate or increase the cap on taxable income.

The BBB tax restores Social Security to financial health primarily by (1) eliminating the cap on taxable income, and (2) earmarking all payroll tax revenue for Social Security (none is diverted to fund Medicare since the VAT funds Medicare Choice).

Comparison of Tax Reform Alternatives (continued)

Discretionary spending: Six of the alternatives increase discretionary spending over the next 10 years compared to current policy. Most of the proposed increase is for education, infrastructure, defense, green investments, and social programs. One of the alternatives does not increase discretionary spending relative to current policy.

The BBB tax increases discretionary spending compared to current policy. Part of this increase is earmarked for education and infrastructure, but most is left to the discretion of Congress and the president.

Climate change: Six of the seven alternatives include carbon taxes. The BBB tax includes carbon dividends, which are similar to carbon taxes except all revenue is rebated to the American public with quarterly or monthly dividend checks.

Bipartisanship: Six of the tax reform alternatives are not bipartisan. The three on the left side of Table 6-5, which were proposed by right-leaning think tanks, are not bipartisan because they eliminate Medicare and replace it with a "premium support" system. Most liberals reject this approach because they fear it will leave low-income and moderate-income taxpayers with inadequate health care.

The three tax reforms on the right side of Table 6-5, which were proposed by left-leaning think tanks, are not bipartisan because they significantly increase tax rates. Most conservatives reject high tax rates. They also dislike the Medicare-for-All plans included in two of these alternatives because they lack strong cost controls and have no opt-out provision.

The Bipartisan Policy Center proposal can potentially achieve bipartisan support. It is an incremental improvement to the current tax code, which is aimed primarily at reducing federal deficits and restoring Social Security to financial health. While this proposal may achieve bipartisan support, it is not fundamental tax reform. That is not a criticism; rather, it is an observation, based on knowing that sometimes incremental change is best.

The BBB tax can potentially achieve bipartisan support because it achieves the most important objectives of conservatives, liberals, moderates, and independents.

Summary: The BBB tax is unique because it is a fundamental and comprehensive tax reform that is also bipartisan. This illustrates why SE is so powerful—it encourages the development of radically new and better "systems solutions" that are nonpartisan because they address the needs and desires of all stakeholders.

The BBB Tax Is Better than the Current Tax Code and the Seven Alternative Tax Reform Proposals

Table 6-6 summarizes my evaluation of the BBB tax versus the current tax code and the seven tax reform alternatives. You are encouraged to perform your own evaluation. The basis for my evaluation is discussed below and on the following page.

Fiscally responsible: The current tax code is rated very poor (2 out of 10) because its large deficits are rapidly increasing the national debt. The BBB tax and all seven tax reform alternatives are rated much better because they substantially reduce the deficit. The BBB tax and the AAF proposal are rated good (8 out of 10) because they balance the budget. The three proposals that nearly balance the budget are rated slightly lower (7 out of 10) and the three that do not balance the budget are rated lower (5 out of 7).

Pro-growth: The current tax code is rated good (8 out of 10) because it has low tax rates. The BBB tax and the four tax reform alternatives that maintain low tax rates are also rated good (8 out of 10). The three tax reform alternatives that significantly increase individual and corporate income tax rates are rated poor (4 out of 10).

Realistic: The current tax code, the BBB tax, and all tax reform alternatives are rated good (4 out of 5) since they have all been evaluated with realistic assumptions.

Table 6-6. Summary Comparison of Alternative Tax Systems

Objective	Maximum Points	Current Tax Code (TCJA)	BBB Tax	Evaluation of Tax Reform Alternatives						
				AAF	AEI	MI	BPC	PPI	CAP	EPI
Fiscally responsible	10	2	8	8	7	5	5	7	5	7
Pro-growth	10	8	8	8	8	8	8	4	4	4
Realistic	5	4	4	4	4	4	4	4	4	4
Comprehensive	5	2	5	4	4	4	4	4	4	4
Fair	10	2	8	4	4	4	6	6	7	7
Simple	5	2	4	3	3	3	3	3	3	3
Permanent	5	2	4	4	4	4	4	4	4	4
Bipartisan	10	4	8	4	4	4	8	4	4	4
Total	60	26	49	39	38	36	42	36	35	37

Source: The author prepared this table. You are encouraged to do your own evaluation.
Key: Very good = 5 out of 5 or 10 out of 10   Good = 4 out of 5 or 8 out of 10
    Fair = 3 out of 5 or 6 out of 10   Poor = 2 out of 5 or 4 out of 10
    Very poor = 1 out of 5 or 2 out of 10   Unacceptable = 0 out of 5 or 0 out of 10

The BBB Tax Is Better Than the Current Tax Code
and the Seven Alternative Tax Reform Proposals (continued)

Comprehensive: The current tax code is rated poor (2 out of 5) because it fails to address many urgent problems. The BBB tax is rated very good (5 out of 5) because it addresses all major issues with the current tax code. The other seven tax reform alternatives are rated good (4 out of 5) because they address most issues with the current tax code.

Fair: The current tax code is rated very poor (2 out of 10) because it provides a poor health care system that leaves many taxpayers economically vulnerable, a Social Security system that is not sustainable, many tax preferences and loopholes, and limited opportunities for low-income and middle-income taxpayers to move up the income ladder. The BBB tax is rated good (8 out of 10) because it taxes all income at the same (progressive) rate, improves the health care system, makes Social Security sustainable, provides cash payments to all taxpayers (income tax credits and carbon dividends), and increases investment in education and infrastructure. The alternatives that provide Medicare-for-All are rated slightly lower (7 out of 10). Those that continue the current health care system with minor upgrades are rated fair (6 out of 10) and those that replace Medicare with a premium support system are rated poor (4 out of 10).

Simple: The current tax code is rated poor (2 out of 5) because it is very complex. The BBB tax is rated good (4 out of 5) because it is much simpler. The seven tax reform alternatives are all rated fair (3 out of 5) because they are simpler than the current tax code but more complex than the BBB tax.

Permanent: The current tax code is rated poor (2 out of 5) because it is not permanent. The BBB tax and the seven alternatives are rated good (4 out of 5) because they are all permanent.

Bipartisan: The current tax code is rated poor (4 out of 10) because it is not bipartisan. The BBB tax and the Bipartisan Policy Center (BPC) proposal are rated good (8 out of 10) because they can potentially achieve bipartisan support. The other six tax reform proposals are rated poor (4 out of 10) because they are not bipartisan.

Summary: The numbers in this table are subjective and are less important than the insights gained while performing the evaluation. Nevertheless, the summary values at the bottom of this table suggest to me two conclusions. First, the BBB tax and all of the alternatives are better than the current tax code. Second, the BBB tax is better than any of the alternatives. You can draw your own conclusions.

7 TAX REFORM ROADMAP

Tax reform will not just magically happen. Lawmakers need a systematic process to develop and implement tax reform and continuously improve the tax code.

The best way to do this is for Congress to establish a new organization to develop and recommend nonpartisan tax reform. This new organization could also develop and recommend nonpartisan solutions to other urgent national problems. This organization could be patterned after the Congressional Budget Office (CBO), a bipartisan organization that supports Congress by providing data and analysis relating to the budget. However, unlike the CBO, the charter for this new organization would be to develop nonpartisan solutions for Congress and the president to consider.

This new organization might also be patterned after the SE organizations in companies that develop complex products such as aircraft and spacecraft. However, instead of developing physical products and systems, this new organization would develop nonpartisan solutions to social, economic, and political problems. This organization might be named the Nonpartisan Solutions Office (NSO) because its charter would be to use SE and other fact-based and data-driven methods to develop practical nonpartisan solutions that could serve as the starting point for debate in Congress.

The following pages describe one approach for how this organization could help Congress and the president address tax reform.

SE Process for Tax Reform

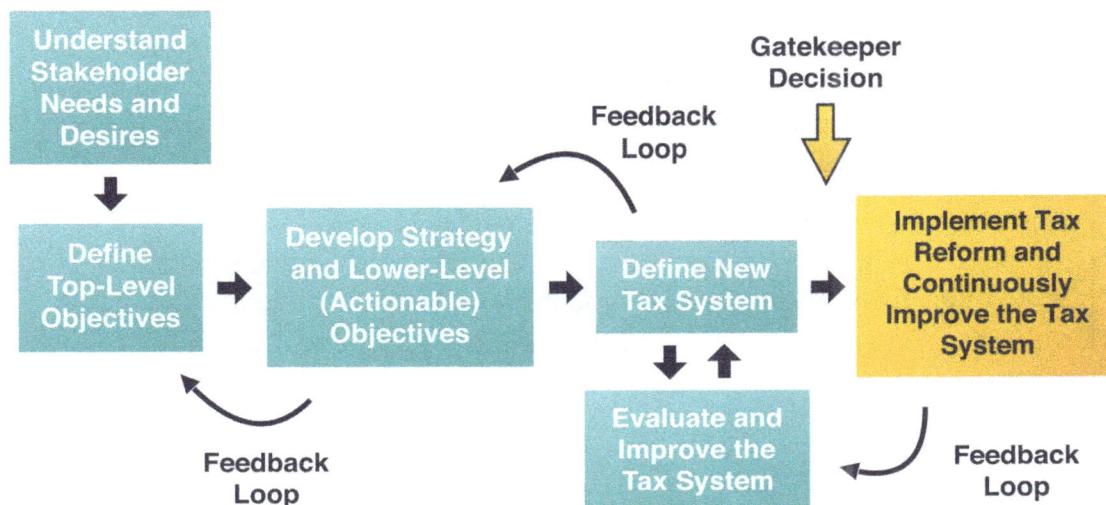

Year #1 Work Scope

The Nonpartisan Solutions Office (NSO) should perform the following work scope in the first year, with support from specialists in other organizations such as the JCT (Joint Committee on Taxation) and the CBO (Congressional Budget Office):

- Define objectives for tax reform.

- Develop several "candidate" tax systems.

- Evaluate the candidate tax systems against the objectives.

- Select the "best" tax system (or systems) for further investigation.

- Develop a tax reform proposal for Congress to consider.

- Submit a report to Congress in December of the first year with (1) proposed objectives for tax reform, (2) candidate tax systems, (3) evaluation of these candidates, and (4) recommendations for tax reform.

Congress should request comments from a wide range of stakeholders on the proposed tax reform.

Initially, the NSO charter should include just a few of the highest priority national issues such as tax reform, health care, immigration, climate change, and the justice system.

Over time, the NSO charter might be expanded to address other key national problems. Eventually, the NSO charter might include 10 or more subjects. Since many national and international problems are interrelated, the NSO should consider not only the optimum solution for each problem, but also how the proposed solutions are interrelated. In other words, the NSO should take a "system of systems" approach when developing their proposed solutions.

The NSO is not a policymaking organization. That is the role of Congress and the president. The NSO charter is only to evaluate alternatives and develop nonpartisan proposals for Congress and the president to consider.

Work Scope in Year #2 and Following Years

Work scope in year #2:

Congress should conduct hearings on the proposed tax reform and either pass a comprehensive tax reform bill or defer action to the following year.

If Congress and the president do not enact comprehensive tax reform, the NSO should repeat the year #1 work scope, based on comments received and insights gained during the congressional hearing process. The year #2 work scope would be as follows:

- Update the objectives for tax reform.

- Improve the "candidate" tax systems.

- Evaluate the candidate tax systems against the objectives.

- Develop a new tax reform proposal for Congress to consider.

- Submit a report to Congress in December with (1) updated objectives for tax reform, (2) improved candidate tax systems, (3) evaluation of these candidates, and (4) recommendations for tax reform.

Congress should request comments on the proposed tax reform.

Work scope in year #3 and following years:

The year #2 scope of work should be repeated each year until Congress and the president implement fundamental tax reform.

This process should result in increasingly attractive tax reform proposals until one proposal achieves strong bipartisan support.

Repeating this process annually will make tax reform a normal, routine process rather than a one-time event. This will reduce political posturing and allow rational discussion of alternatives. When tax reform discussions become routine, compromise will be possible and rational tax reform will be achievable.

Continuous Improvement

Figure 7-1 illustrates how continuous improvement has changed aircraft design over the past 80 years. Imagine how great the tax code would be today if it had been continuously improved for the past 80 years like aircraft!

Congress should establish a continuous improvement process for the tax system. For example, the NSO could perform the following work scope each year:

- Update the objectives for tax reform.

- Identify changes that could potentially improve the tax system.

- Evaluate these candidate changes against the objectives.

- Identify changes that improve the tax code.

- Submit a report to Congress in December with (1) updated objectives for tax reform, (2) changes they evaluated to improve the tax system, (3) results of their evaluation, and (4) recommended improvements (if any).

Congress should request comments on the proposed changes, conduct hearings, and approve those that have strong bipartisan support.

Repeating this process annually will continuously improve the tax code and make tax reform a continuous, rational process rather than an infrequent, irrational event.

Figure 7-1. Continuous Improvement Drives Economic Growth

The **Boeing 80** was America's first airliner designed to transport passengers on a scheduled service. Introduced in 1928, it carried 18 passengers at 125 miles per hour. It had three piston engines and its fuselage was covered in fabric.

Photo used with Boeing's permission.

The **Boeing 787** was introduced in 2011. It carries 242 to 440 passengers at 560 miles per hour. It has two jet engines, its fuselage and wings are made of carbon fiber composites, and it can fly non-stop up to 8,800 miles.

Photo used with Boeing's permission.

8 SUMMARY AND NEXT STEPS

President Kennedy challenged America in his inaugural address: "Ask not what your country can do for you—ask what you can do for your country."

Lawmakers, taxpayers, and special interests should heed his advice and "ask not what the tax system can do for you—ask what the tax system can do for America."

We need a tax system that works for all Americans: a simple, efficient, and fair tax system that encourages economic growth, expands opportunities, creates jobs, promotes shared prosperity, and protects the environment.

Too often, lawmakers have optimized the tax system to promote special interests and favored constituents. This has sub-optimized the overall tax system. As a result, the tax system is a mess.

Lawmakers should optimize the tax system for all Americans. This is the best way for them to serve their constituents and, ironically, special interests.

This is not the only reason to fix the tax system. Our forefathers established the United States based on the idea that democracy and free markets are the best path to freedom and prosperity. Now, democracy and free markets are being challenged around the world by dictators, strongmen, terrorists, ultra-nationalists, isolationists, and many others.

We cannot win the battle for the hearts and minds of the world with weapons. We can win it only by fixing America's problems so others will be attracted to democracy, freedom, and free markets. This requires fundamental tax reform.

Nations have risen and fallen throughout history. Success is never guaranteed but must be continually earned. We must fix our broken tax system to maintain and enhance our position in the world.

America should accept nothing less than the world's best tax system. If we can send astronauts to the moon and return them safely, surely we can fix the tax system. Failure is not an option.

Key Features of the BBB Tax

Following is a summary of the key features of the BBB tax. Nearly all of these features have been used (successfully) in other countries. Nevertheless, the BBB tax is unique—not because its features are new, but because of the way they are combined using the principles of systems engineering into an integrated, nonpartisan tax system.

Individual income tax: The BBB income tax is a progressive tax, yet its top tax rate is low (36%). Because it is a progressive tax, it partially addresses the problem of income and wealth inequality. Just as important, low tax rates encourage economic growth and create jobs.

VAT (health care): The corporate income tax is eliminated and replaced with a VAT with a low tax rate (13%). The VAT is an economically efficient tax that provides sufficient revenue to fund Medicare Choice. Eliminating the corporate income tax will stimulate business investment and create jobs.

Payroll tax (Social Security): The payroll tax rate is decreased to 14%, yet it provides sufficient revenue to fully fund Social Security. This is achieved by eliminating the cap on taxable income, earmarking all payroll tax revenue for Social Security (no diversion for Medicare), and taxing all Social Security benefits as ordinary income.

Carbon dividends: The BBB tax includes revenue-neutral carbon dividends. They are an economically efficient way to address climate change. Carbon dividends also provide cash payments to all taxpayers and make the tax system more progressive.

Balanced budgets: The BBB tax balances the federal budget. This will slowly decrease the national debt as a percent of GDP. An automatic feedback mechanism is included to encourage Congress and the president to control spending.

Investment in future growth: The BBB tax increases investment in education and infrastructure. It does this by increasing funding for the Highway and Mass Transit Trust Funds and creating (and funding) an Education Trust Fund.

Tax transparency: Candidates for high-level public office are required to disclose their tax returns. This is done to promote good governance and reduce corruption.

Inequality: The BBB tax addresses the problem of inequality in four ways. First, it is a progressive tax. Second, it provides a strong social safety net. Third, it increases investment in education and infrastructure. Fourth, it will stimulate economic growth and create jobs, especially for low-income and middle-income taxpayers.

Next Steps

Many organizations, groups, and individuals have proposed tax reforms in the past 20 years, but none has achieved strong bipartisan support. So why might *Rational Tax Reform* stimulate action now? There are three major reasons for optimism.

First, *Rational Tax Reform* is different from other tax reforms proposed in the past 20 years because it is not just a tax reform proposal (the BBB tax). It is also a multi-year bipartisan process (SE) to develop and implement tax reform. This is codified in the following equation:

Rational Tax Reform = BBB + SE

where:

- BBB = bipartisan balanced budget tax (the starting point for bipartisan tax reform)

- SE = systems engineering (the process to implement bipartisan tax reform)

Second, *Rational Tax Reform* is radical and transformative. Other proposed tax reforms have been more incremental. Bold ideas often excite and motivate people. *Rational Tax Reform* could make the United States a much better country by balancing the federal budget, strengthening the social safety net, and providing a solid foundation for future economic growth. By reducing tax avoidance, tax evasion, and political corruption, it could help restore the public's faith in government.

Third, there is a growing consensus that the current tax system needs to be scrapped and replaced by something much better. Warren Buffet has been preaching for years that the current tax system is unfair. Many other prominent Americans have joined him in the past few years to express dissatisfaction with the current tax system. Yet nobody has proposed a compelling tax reform plan to fill this market need. *Rational Tax Reform* satisfies this unmet need and can give hope and inspiration to those who think tax reform is a lost cause.

The next two pages discuss what it will take for Americans to throw off the shackles of the current tax code and move to a much better tax system.

Who Will Lead?

Tax reform will not happen unless Americans overwhelmingly support and demand it. That will require a national discussion. There are many people who could lead this discussion. Here are a few:

Presidential candidates: The upcoming presidential election will stimulate debate on many issues. Tax reform should be one of them. One or more candidates could draw favorable attention to themselves and advance the national interest by promoting bipartisan tax reform.

Business leaders: Many business leaders are dissatisfied with the current tax code. People such as Warren Buffet, Michael Bloomberg, Bill Gates, and Howard Schultz could encourage bipartisan tax reform.

Non-profit organizations: Many non-profit organizations, such as the Tax Policy Center, the Peter G. Peterson Foundation, the Bipartisan Policy Center, the Tax Foundation, the Center on Budget and Policy Priorities, the American Enterprise Institute, the Economic Policy Institute, and the Center for American Progress are concerned about the growing national debt. Although these organizations span the political spectrum, they all support tax reform. They could lead a national dialogue on tax reform.

Congress: The current Congress needs to do something significant to show Americans that they can work together and pass bipartisan legislation. A good first step would be to form a bipartisan "Tax Reform Caucus" to promote nonpartisan tax reform. Their goal should not be to agree on a specific tax reform proposal, but to establish a process to achieve nonpartisan tax reform. The process described in Chapter 7 could be the starting point for their discussions.

Media opinion leaders: There are hundreds of media opinion leaders who could lead or participate in a national debate on tax reform. Three examples are (1) editorial staff at major newspapers such as the *New York Times,* the *Wall Street Journal,* and the *Washington Post;* (2) economic commentators on television and radio (such as Steve Rattner on *Morning Joe*); and (3) television and film producers (such as Ken Burns, who could undoubtedly produce a compelling documentary on tax reform).

State lawmakers: Many states need to reform their tax codes. Some state lawmakers are already interested in tax reform. An example is Governor Gavin Newsom of California. The SE process is as applicable to state tax codes as it is to the federal tax code. So, perhaps one or more state lawmakers will take the lead to implement bipartisan tax reform in their states without waiting for the federal government to act.

Who Will Lead? (continued)

Aspiring political leaders: Both political parties are undergoing significant change. Many aspiring leaders are searching for meaningful ways to lead their parties into the future. Hyper-partisanship has created a gap in the middle for centrist ideas. Aspiring politicians could distinguish themselves by promoting bipartisan tax reform, just as President Reagan did in his second term.

Medicare-for-All supporters: Many Americans support Medicare-for-All. The best way for them to achieve their objective of universal health care may be to support tax reform as a means to achieve health care reform.

Former political leaders: Many retired political leaders have promoted special causes. Bipartisan tax reform could be a good cause for energetic, respected former politicians.

Concerned citizens: You and I can also make a difference. I wrote this book to help jump-start a discussion on tax reform. You can contribute to this conversation as follows:

- **Personal contacts:** Talk to your friends and relatives about tax reform. Give them your copy of this book. Send an email to your friends or post a message on social media. If you know one or more prominent opinion leaders and change-makers, talk to them and give them your copy of this book.

- **Media:** You can publicize the need for tax reform through social media. If you are an editor, reporter, contributor, host, or leader in print, broadcast, the Internet, or social media, you can add your voice to the national discussion. I intend to actively promote nonpartisan tax reform. You can find creative and interesting ways to express your views on tax reform and inform Americans about the need for action.

- **Crowdsourcing:** We can crowdsource tax reform. After you read this book, post a review on Amazon. Describe what you like and dislike about the BBB tax and the SE process. Provide your opinions on tax reform. If you are in a book club, read this book with your club and post a review with your combined comments. Politicians, policymakers, and anyone else will then be able to read the Amazon book reviews and learn what a broad cross-section of Americans think about tax reform. If enough reviews and comments are posted, I will develop a second edition of this book.

The longest journey begins with a single step. The path to tax reform is long. So we must begin now, with urgency, to achieve bipartisan tax reform before it is too late.

9 BEYOND TAX REFORM

As mentioned previously, the SE process can (and should) be used to address other societal problems in addition to tax reform. Following is my list of America's twelve most serious problems and some thoughts on how SE can help resolve them:

- **Health care:** The goal of health care reform should be to improve health care, reduce cost, and provide universal coverage. Health care reform should address all health care issues, including mental health, drug abuse, reproductive health care, abortion, and end-of-life decisions. Medicare Choice can be the starting point for developing comprehensive health care reform.

- **Wars and terrorism:** A global strategy is needed to reduce wars and terrorism, including (and especially) the risk of nuclear war. This is an immense challenge, since history suggests that violence is ingrained in human nature. Nevertheless, SE could provide a logical framework for global discussions to address this issue.

- **Climate change:** This is one of the world's most serious problems, yet the world has been unable to agree on how to adequately address it. SE can help develop a practical plan to address climate change without damaging the economy. Carbon dividends can be the starting point for developing a cost-effective, global climate change policy.

- **Economic inequality:** Comprehensive reforms are needed to address the root causes and consequences of economic inequality, such as inadequate education, lack of job opportunities, poverty, homelessness, and food insecurity. The BBB tax will help reduce economic inequality, but it is only a small step in the right direction.

- **Social inequality:** Social inequality is closely linked to economic inequality. Fundamental reform is needed to address the root causes of explicit and implicit discrimination on the basis of race, religion, gender, and other factors.

- **Justice system:** We incarcerate too many people for too long, yet there is too much crime and those who serve time are often unprepared to re-enter society when they are released. A key goal of justice system reform should be to address the root causes of crime, violence, incarceration, and recidivism.

- **Immigration policy:** Immigration reform should consider the needs of all Americans (including recent immigrants), prospective immigrants, and other countries. Immigration policy should protect and enhance culture, identity, freedom, and economic opportunity.

- **Education:** America's education system is great for the brightest and most privileged students. However, it leaves too many students behind. The goal of education reform should be to ensure that all students have an opportunity to receive a good education at an affordable price and learn what they need to know to become good, productive, and happy citizens.

Beyond Tax Reform (continued)

- **Governance policy:** America's governance policies are outdated. They need to be updated to promote good governance and eliminate the root causes of corruption. Reform is especially needed to improve campaign financing, ensure fair elections, and reduce patronage, especially appointments given to campaign donors and lobbyists.

- **International relations:** America's foreign policy is often inconsistent, ineffective, and counterproductive. A coherent long-term vision is needed to guide global governance, globalization, and bilateral and multilateral policy decisions. This vision should consider all stakeholders and integrate political, economic, and security considerations.

- **Environmental sustainability:** America enacted landmark reforms in the past few decades to promote clean air and clean water. However, much more remains to be done, both domestically and internationally, to protect the environment. Reform is especially needed to (1) protect the world's oceans and biodiversity, and (2) use water, soil, and other natural resources sustainably. Environmental sustainability is closely linked to climate change, but climate change should be treated as a separate issue because of its uniqueness and importance.

- **Tax reform:** The tax system is a root cause of many of America's most serious economic, social, and political problems. To address these problems, we must eliminate the root cause. This requires fundamental and comprehensive tax reform. The BBB tax can be the starting point for developing comprehensive tax reform.

These problems are the tip of an immense iceberg. Thousands of societal problems need resolution at the national, international, state, and local levels. You may be thinking that some problems are just too controversial to resolve. However, my experience with systems engineering of complex products is that the SE process can help resolve even controversial, polarizing issues if the following two guidelines are followed:

Define the problem broadly. Each problem should be defined broadly enough to enable development of a "system solution." For example, many people may support the BBB tax even though it includes features they do not like, if it contains more features they like. The top twelve problems have purposefully been defined broadly, so the most controversial issues (such as abortion and gun control) are embedded in them and can be viewed in a broader context.

Avoid arbitrary deadlines. Some problems take time to develop good solutions. Experience has taught us that when SE fails (for example, when designing an aircraft), it is usually because a deadline forces adoption of a half-baked solution. The SE process should be allowed several iterations to develop a good solution, especially for complex and controversial problems. The key to success is to repeat the first five steps of the SE process as often as needed to develop a good solution, and to continue repeating the first five steps thereafter to continuously improve the solution.

SE Process for Societal Problems

To achieve its full potential as a tool for addressing societal problems, SE must be reduced to a simple, repeatable process. Figure 9-1 shows a slightly modified version of the SE process used for tax reform. This process can be applied to any social, economic, or political problem. It is effective (and nonpartisan) for the following reasons:

Steps #1 and #2 require anyone using this process to put aside ideology, at least for a while, and focus on understanding the needs and desires of all stakeholders, and synthesizing these needs and desires into top-level objectives. This broadens the mind and increases empathy for opposing viewpoints.

Step #3 requires creative thinking to develop a strategy that achieves all top-level objectives, at least partially. This forces one to reject ideological strategies that focus on just one or two objectives.

Steps #4 and #5 use the strategy developed in step #3 to define a specific solution and evaluate that solution against the objectives and other potential solutions. This forces one to consider alternatives, address deficiencies in the chosen solution, and improve the proposed solution. Often, this leads to changing the strategy developed in step #3.

Step #6 is implemented only after a gatekeeper (such as Congress and the president) agree that the solution is ready for implementation. The gatekeeper must be different from those developing the solution, to provide a check and balance. The first five steps are repeated periodically until the gatekeeper approves implementation—and after that to continuously improve the system.

Figure 9-1. The SE Process for Societal Problems

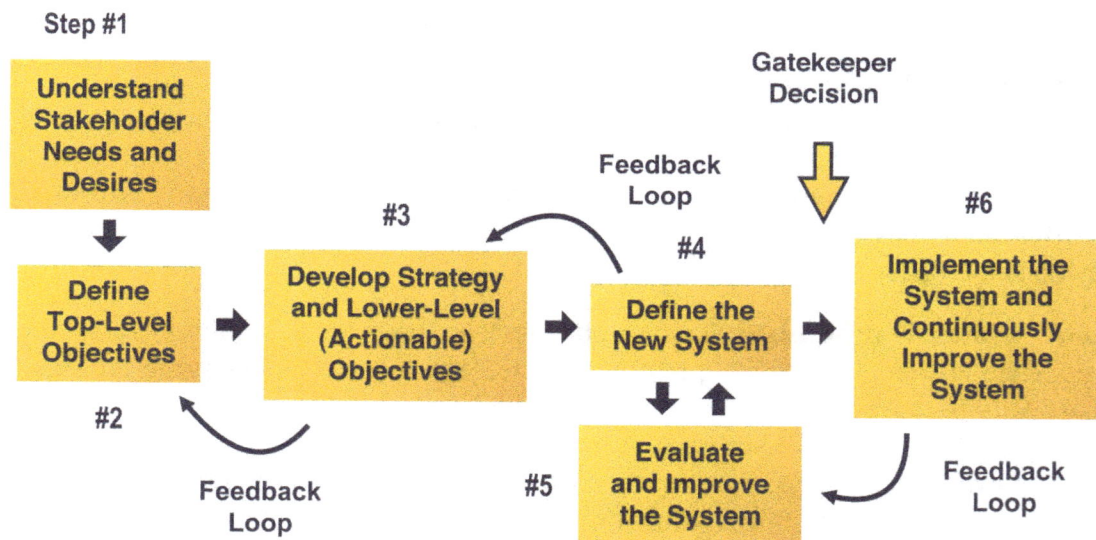

SE for a Better America

America is in trouble. We are deeply divided, and our leaders seem unable to bring us together and tackle many of our most serious problems. SE by itself will not solve our problems, but it can provide a logical framework for evaluating issues and developing nonpartisan solutions. The following actions can help bridge the partisan divide:

- Every legislative body should have one or more organizations such as the Nonpartisan Solutions Office (NSO) described in Chapter 7 to develop nonpartisan proposals. Many legislative bodies already have such an organization; those who do not are often dysfunctional. Without an officially sanctioned organization to develop nonpartisan solutions, most political debates will degenerate into partisan bickering. Using an entity such as an NSO, legislative bodies will at least have nonpartisan "candidate" solutions to consider as the starting point in their deliberations.

- Lawmakers, policymakers, and policy analysts should use SE when developing public policies. Of course, while politicians are campaigning for office, they should express and promote their (often partisan) ideas so voters can form their opinions about the best path forward. However, once elected, leaders should consider everyone's needs and find nonpartisan solutions whenever possible. Wherever you stand on the political spectrum, SE can help you develop and promote fair and balanced solutions without abandoning your core beliefs or alienating your core supporters.

- Educators should teach the SE process. SE is a way of thinking that makes us better citizens. It encourages empathy, promotes respect for others' opinions, requires creative thinking, and teaches fact-based and data-driven reasoning. Students can learn the SE process by working on a team developing a nonpartisan solution to a societal problem. The problem and the team can be as small or as large as time and resources permit.

- Everyone should vote for politicians who will consider the needs of all stakeholders when making public policy, and who articulate specific plans (such as SE) for bringing us together for the common good. This is especially important for far-left and far-right candidates, who tend to be more ideological than centrist candidates.

You can use SE in your daily life. It is a powerful way to think about everyday problems, such as one encounters when developing a long-term relationship, raising children, working as part of a team, or providing a product or service to a customer. SE can help you achieve your goals, whatever they may be. You do not need to be a systems engineer or rigorously adhere to the six-step SE process. You just have to be willing to consider the needs of all stakeholders—and apply facts and data systematically and with common sense—to find optimum solutions.

Conclusion

The two most important actions needed to implement the SE process are as follows: First, Congress should create an organization that will use SE to develop and propose nonpartisan solutions for societal problems. Second, Congress and the president should review and discuss the proposals produced by this new organization in good faith, with the objective of enacting practical, nonpartisan solutions.

The new organization's proposed solution for each societal problem should be updated at least annually until Congress and the president enact a solution, and thereafter to continuously improve the solution. Repeating the process annually will promote rational, fact-based, and data-driven discussion of alternatives.

If Congress and the president use SE to address societal problems, their example can be replicated at all levels in the political process. This is not a pipe dream. If engineers can work together to develop complex products on highly political programs such as the International Space Station, why can't Congress and the president work together to address America's most serious problems? They just need a better process—the SE process.

People in other countries will also notice if Congress and the president begin using SE to address complex societal problems. SE could be a meme that spreads worldwide and provides a fresh approach to address difficult global, national, regional, and local issues.

In 1961, President Kennedy announced his goal to send Americans to the moon and return them safely before the end of the decade, with these words: "We choose to go to the Moon in this decade and do the other things, not because they are easy, but because they are hard; because that goal will serve to organize and measure the best of our energies and skills, because that challenge is one that we are willing to accept, one we are unwilling to postpone, and one we intend to win."

When President Kennedy articulated this goal, many in Congress were skeptical. However, they supported the effort, because they realized America could not afford to lose the space race.

Now, many in Congress may be skeptical about the SE process. However, they should embrace SE because America cannot continue on the current path and lose the battle for the hearts and minds of our citizens, and the hearts and minds of the world.

SE helped America win the space race. Now, SE can help bridge the partisan divide and fix our broken political system. We must show by our actions that we can solve our problems. Divided we will fail—but united, there is no limit to what we can achieve.

Visit JimHartung.com to learn how you can help convince Congress and the president to use the SE process.

GLOSSARY

Alternative minimum tax (AMT): A special tax intended to prevent wealthy taxpayers from taking advantage of so many tax breaks that they pay little or no taxes.

BBB tax: The bipartisan balanced budget tax.

Bureau of Economic Analysis (BEA): The BEA is an agency for the federal government that provides official statistics on economic topics such as GDP, consumer spending, income and saving, prices and inflation, and employment.

Capital gain: Profit from the sale or trade of a property such as a stock or real estate.

Congressional Budget Office (CBO): The CBO is a federal agency within the legislative branch that provides budget and economic information for Congress.

Deduction: An amount subtracted from income before calculating taxes owed.

Dependent: A child or relative that a taxpayer supports. IRS rules for who qualifies as a dependent are quite complicated.

Earned income tax credit (EITC): A refundable tax credit targeted at low-income and moderate-income workers.

Estate tax: A tax on the value of an estate that exceeds a certain amount.

Excise tax: A special tax on using or selling certain products or services.

Federal budget: The federal budget is the government's estimate of revenue and spending for each fiscal year.

Fringe benefit: Compensation given to an employee by an employer in addition to regular pay.

Gift tax: Tax paid by a giver of a gift (money or property) that exceeds a certain amount.

Gross domestic product (GDP): GDP is the value of all the finished goods and services produced within a country's borders in a specific time period. The U.S. GDP in 2018 was about $20 trillion. GDP is measured it two ways: (1) by adding all income received (the income method) and (2) by adding all expenditures (the expenditure method). Table G-1 shows GDP in 2018 as measured by each of these two methods.

Table G-1. GDP Is Measured by Two Methods

How Measured?	% of GDP
Income Method	
- Employee compensation	53%
- Profits and proprietors' income	17%
- Rental and interest income	7%
- Taxes on production and imports (net)	7%
- Depreciation	16%
Total	100%
Expenditure Method	
- Personal consumption	68%
- Private domestic investment	18%
- Government expenditures	17%
- Net exports (exports minus imports)	-3%
Total	100%

Source: Bureau of Economic Analysis, *Gross Domestic Product, Fourth Quarter and Annual 2018 (Initial Estimate)*, February 28, 2019. Compiled by the author.

Head of household: A filing status claimed by taxpayers who are single and have qualifying dependents.

Joint Committee on Taxation (JCT): The JCT is a nonpartisan committee that supports both parties and both houses of Congress on tax legislation. It is composed of ten members (five from the Senate Finance Committee and five from the House Ways and Means Committee) and it has a staff of economists, attorneys, and accountants.

Married filing jointly: A filing status claimed by married couples who wish to combine income and file a single tax return together.

Married filing separately: A filing status claimed by married couples who do not wish to file a joint return and agree to report their income separately.

Medicaid: A joint federal and state program that helps pay medical costs for some people with limited income and resources. Medicaid programs vary from state to state.

Medicare: Health care insurance that the federal government provides for Americans aged 65 and older. It also covers younger people with (1) qualifying disabilities, (2) end-stage renal disease (kidney disease requiring dialysis), and (3) amyotrophic lateral sclerosis (ALS). Medicare includes two major alternatives as follows:

- **Original Medicare:** This is the original "fee-for-service" health plan offered by Medicare. Under this plan, patients select their health care providers and pay their share of the cost; Medicare pays its share of the cost.

- **Medicare Advantage:** This is an alternative to original Medicare. Under this plan, patients may choose an HMO (health maintenance organization) or PPO (preferred provider organization) to provide comprehensive health care.

Medicare-for-All: One way to provide universal health care, by expanding Medicare to include all age groups. This approach is favored by many progressive Democrats.

Medicare Choice: Another way to provide universal health care, which is proposed here. Medicare Choice is similar to Medicare-for-All, but it includes strong cost controls and an opt-out provision.

National debt: The amount of debt owed to others by the U.S. Treasury. Table G-2 shows this in two categories: (1) debt held by the public (including foreign governments), and (2) debt held by other agencies of the federal government. At the end of 2018, the debt owed to the public was 78% of GDP (about $16 trillion) and the total debt was 106% of GDP (about $22 trillion). In 2019, the total debt increased to $23 trillion.

Table G-2. U.S. National Debt at End of 2018

Who Owns the National Debt?	% of GDP
Debt Owed to the Public	78%
- Foreign governments and investors (40%)	
- Domestic investors, including Federal Reserve (60%)	
Debt Owed to Other Federal Agencies	28%
- Social Security Trust Fund (50%)	
- Government employee and military retirement funds (36%)	
- Cash and other trust funds (14%)	
Total (gross national debt)	106%

Source: Congressional Budget Office, *The Budget and Economic Outlook 2019 to 2029*, January 2019. Compiled by the author.

Nonpartisan Solutions Office (NSO): A new organization proposed in this book. It would assist Congress by developing nonpartisan solutions for tax reform and other urgent social, economic, and political problems.

Payroll tax: A tax on wages, salaries, and some fringe benefits. It is usually imposed on both employers and employees.

Premium support: This is an alternative to Medicare, which many conservatives are promoting as a way to reduce health care costs and increase competition. With premium support, the government does not provide Medicare coverage, but instead provides each person with money they can use to purchase their own insurance. If a person wishes to purchase insurance that costs more than the support provided by the government, that person must pay the difference. Many liberals dislike this approach because they fear the government will provide insufficient funds for low-income and middle-income taxpayers to obtain adequate health care insurance.

Refundable tax credit: A tax credit that is paid to taxpayers whether or not tax is owed.

Roth IRA: A special Individual Retirement Account (IRA) in which contributions are not tax deductible but interest and withdrawals are tax-free after reaching retirement age.

Single filing status: A filing status claimed by those who are unmarried, divorced, or legally separated and who do not qualify for head of household.

Social Security: The U.S. government program that pays benefits to retirees, workers who become disabled, and survivors of deceased workers. The retirement benefit received depends on the average monthly earnings during the 35 highest-earning years. Retirement may begin as early as age 62 at a discounted rate, and the amount received increases each year that benefits are delayed until the recipient is 70 years old. Spouses are also eligible for benefits even if they have limited or no work histories.

Systems engineering (SE): A systematic, multi-disciplinary approach for the design, development, implementation, and operation of a system. SE seeks a balanced design in the face of opposing interests and many, often conflicting objectives and constraints.

Tax avoidance: Using legal tax planning strategies to reduce taxes owed.

Tax Cuts and Jobs Act (TCJA) of 2017: This is the most recent tax reform. It was enacted by the Republicans in Congress and President Trump without bipartisan support.

Tax evasion: Using illegal means to reduce taxes owed.

Tax Reform Act of 1986: A bipartisan tax reform enacted by Congress and President Reagan. It was the last major tax reform prior to the Tax Cuts and Jobs Act of 2017.

Value-added tax (VAT): A consumption tax levied on the value added to a product or service during each stage of its production or distribution.

LIST OF FIGURES AND TABLES

BIBLIOGRAPHY

Books on Tax Reform

1. Reid, T. R., *A Fine Mess: A Global Quest for a Simpler, Fairer, and More Efficient Tax System* (Penguin Books, New York, 2018).

2. Saez, Emmanuel and Gabriel Zucman, *The Triumph of Injustice, How the Rich Dodge Taxes and How to Make Them Pay* (W. W. Horton and Company, New York, 2019).

3. Gale, William G., *Fiscal Therapy: Curing America's Debt Addiction and Investing in the Future* (Oxford University Press, New York, 2019).

4. Bartlett, Bruce, *The Benefit and The Burden: Tax Reform—Why We Need It and What It Will Take* (Simon & Schuster, New York, 2012).

5. Slemrod, Joel and Jon Bakija, *Taxing Ourselves: A Citizen's Guide to the Debate over Taxes* (The MIT Press, 2017).

6. Auerbach, Alan J. and Kent Smetters, *The Economics of Tax Policy* (Oxford University Press, 2017).

Books on Health Care Reform

7. Reid, T. R., *The Healing of America: A Global Quest for Better, Cheaper, and Fairer Health Care* (Penguin Books, New York, 2010).

8. Makary, Marty, *The Price We Pay: What Broke American Health Care—and How to Fix It* (Bloomsbury Publishing, New York, 2019).

Reports and Papers

9. Gale, William G. and Benjamin H. Harris, *A Value-Added Tax for the United States: Part of the Solution*, July 2010, Urban-Brookings Tax Policy Center, Washington, DC.

10. Toder, Eric, Jim Nunns, and Joseph Rosenberg, *Using a VAT to Reform the Income Tax*, January 2012, Urban-Brookings Tax Policy Center, Washington, DC.

11. Toder, Eric, Jim Nunns, and Joseph Rosenberg, *Implications of Different Bases for a VAT*, February 2012, Urban-Brookings Tax Policy Center, Washington, DC.

12. Marron, Donald and Elaine Maag, *How to Design Carbon Dividends*, December 12, 2018, Urban-Brookings Tax Policy Center, Washington, DC.

13. Zucman, Gabriel, *Global Wealth Inequality*, Working Paper 25462, National Bureau of Economic Research, January 2019.

14. Pollin, Robert, James Heintz, Peter Arno, Jeanette Wicks-Lim, and Michael Ash, *Economic Analysis of Medicare for All*, November 2018, Political Economy Research Institute (PERI), University of Massachusetts Amherst.

15. Shrank, William H., Teresa L. Rogstad, and Natasha N. Parekh, *Waste in the US Health Care System: Estimated Costs and Potential for Savings*, JAMA, published online ahead of print version, October 7, 2019.

16. Liu, Jodi L., *Exploring Single-Payer Alternatives for Health Care Reform,* (RAND Corporation, 2016).

17. Horowitz, John, Julie-Anne Cronin, Hannah Hawkins, Laura Konda, and Alex Yuskavage, *Methodology for Analyzing a Carbon Tax*, Office of Tax Analysis Working Paper 115, January 2017, U.S. Department of Treasury.

18. Stockman, Bill, Joe Boyle, and John Bacon, *International Space Station Systems Engineering Case Study*, Air Force Center for Systems Engineering, 2010.

19. U.S. Environmental Protection Agency, *Inventory of U.S. Greenhouse Gas Emissions and Sinks, 1990–2016*, April 2018.

20. Report of the President's Advisory Panel on Federal Tax Reform, *Simple, Fair, and Pro-Growth: Proposals to Fix America's Tax System*, November 2005.

21. National Commission on Fiscal Responsibility and Reform, *The Moment of Truth*, December 2010.

22. Bureau of Economic Analysis, *Gross Domestic Product,* published monthly.

23. Congressional Budget Office, *The Budget and Economic Outlook, 2019 to 2029*, January 2019.

24. Congressional Budget Office, *The 2018 Long-Term Budget Outlook*, June 2018.

25. Congressional Budget Office, *The Long-Term Budget Outlook Under Alternative Scenarios for Fiscal Policy,* August 2018.

26. U.S. Department of the Treasury, *Financial Report of the United States Government,* Fiscal Year 2018.

27. Peter G. Peterson Foundation, *Solutions Initiative 2019: Charting a Sustainable Future*, June 2019.

28. Nystrom, Scott and Patrick Luckow, *The Economic, Climate, Fiscal, Power, and Demographic Impact of a National Fee-and-Dividend Carbon Tax*, REMI (Regional Economic Models, Inc.) and Synapse Energy Economics, Inc., June 2014.

Government Organizations

29. Congressional Budget Office (CBO): https://www.cbo.gov.

30. Bureau of Economic Analysis (BEA): https://www.bea.gov.

31. Centers for Medicare and Medicaid Services (CMS): https://www.cms.gov.

32. Joint Committee on Taxation (JCT): https://www.jct.gov.

33. Internal Revenue Service (IRS) statistics: https://www.irs.gov/statistics.

34. Organization for Economic Cooperation and Development (OECD): OECD.org.

35. Centers for Disease Control and Prevention: https://www.cdc.gov.

Nonprofit Organizations

36. Peter G. Peterson Foundation: https://www.pgpf.org.

37. Tax Policy Center: https://www.taxpolicycenter.org.

38. Tax Foundation: https://taxfoundation.org.

39. Center on Budget and Policy Priorities: https://www.cbpp.org.

40. Institute on Taxation and Economic Policy: https://itep.org.

41. Citizens' Climate Lobby: https://citizensclimatelobby.org.

42. Climate Leadership Council: https://www.clcouncil.org.

43. Bipartisan Policy Center: https://bipartisanpolicy.org.

44. National Bureau of Economic Research (NBER): https://www.nber.org.

ACKNOWLEDGMENTS

This book was inspired and informed by two excellent books by T. R. Reid: *A Fine Mess: A Global Quest for a Simpler, Fairer, and More Efficient Tax System* and *The Healing of America: A Global Quest for Better, Cheaper, and Fairer Health Care*. These books provided a solid foundation for my work.

Systems engineering requires facts and data. Therefore, I am indebted to the many government organizations who collect and analyze data relating to tax policy. Six organizations that deserve special mention are: the Congressional Budget Office (CBO), the Bureau of Economic Analysis (BEA), the Internal Revenue Service (IRS), the Joint Committee on Taxation (JCT), the Organization for Economic Cooperation and Development (OECD), and the Centers for Medicare and Medicaid Services (CMS).

I am also indebted to several non-profit organizations whose analyses contributed to this book. Seven organizations whose work was most important for developing my ideas are: the National Bureau of Economic Research (NBER), the Peter G. Peterson Foundation, the Tax Policy Center, the Tax Foundation, the Center on Budget and Policy Priorities, the Citizens' Climate Lobby, and the Climate Leadership Council. The Peter G. Peterson Foundation has kindly given me permission to use several of their figures in this book.

I am especially grateful to those who reviewed this book and provided feedback prior to publication. The following deserve special mention: Marni MacRae, Stephanie Hoogstad, Kit Duncan, Phil Rutherford, Saif Benjaafar, T. R. Reid, Stacie Frerichs, Jim and Patty Carey, Suzie Housley, Jacques Franco, Whitney Baer, Akinola Osebi James, Maggie Odigie, Bethany Votaw, Joel Feinblatt, Sandy Vattimo, Cynthia Parten, Matt Williams, Ted Heintz, Monica Mann, Ron Piekunka, Max Winters, and Christy Leos.

While I was writing this book, seven public policy organizations independently developed tax reform proposals. They are: the Center for American Progress, the Bipartisan Policy Center, the Manhattan Institute, the American Enterprise Institute, the Economic Policy Institute, the Progressive Policy Institute, and the American Action Forum. Their proposals provided a robust basis for comparing alternative tax reforms— and their commitment to improving the tax code gives me hope that fundamental tax reform is possible.

Special thanks to Stephanie Chandler and her team at Authority Publishing: Lewis Agrell for the cover design, George Mason for editing, Chela Hardy for project management, and last but not least, Stephanie for expert advice throughout the entire process.

Finally, my wonderful wife Carol has provided wise and patient support. She has given me the gift of time and engaged in countless discussions to improve my thinking and clarify my writing. For this and everything else she has given me, I thank her.

ABOUT THE AUTHOR

Jim Hartung has nearly 40 years' experience as a systems engineer, manager, and executive in the aerospace and energy industries. Most of his career he worked at Rocketdyne, which was owned (sequentially) by Rockwell International, Boeing, and United Technologies. As a result, he understands how all these companies perform systems engineering.

Jim received a BS in Physics from the University of Minnesota and an MS in Engineering Management from UCLA. He served as an Engineering Officer in the U.S. Navy for four years, working for Admiral Rickover on the design and operational support of nuclear power plants for submarines and aircraft carriers.

During his career, Jim worked on or led systems engineering for a wide range of projects. As Director of Systems Engineering and Integration for the International Space Station electric power system, he participated in one of the most complex and successful systems engineering activities ever undertaken. As Director of Energy Systems for Rocketdyne, he led development of advanced energy systems and technologies.

The picture on the right, which was given to Jim when he retired, shows some of the systems, programs, and technologies he worked on during his career.

Jim has prepared his own tax returns since he was a teenager. As a result, he understands first-hand the current tax code and how it has evolved over the past 50 years.

Jim developed and pioneered the idea that systems engineering can be used to optimize social, economic, and political systems as well as physical products and systems. His website (jimhartung.com) provides additional information about how systems engineering can be used to address societal problems.